Surprised by Truth 3

Surprised by Truth 3

10 more converts explain the biblical
and historical reasons for becoming Catholic

Edited by
Patrick Madrid

SOPHIA INSTITUTE PRESS®
Manchester, New Hampshire

Sophia Institute Press
Box 5284, Manchester, NH 03108
1-800-888-9344
www.sophiainstitute.com

Library of Congress Cataloging-in-Publication Data

Surprised by truth 3 : 10 more converts explain the biblical
    and historical reasons for becoming Catholic / Patrick
    Madrid, editor.
        p.   cm.
    Includes bibliographical references.
    ISBN 1-928832-59-8 (pbk. : alk. paper)
    1. Catholic converts — Biography. I. Madrid, Patrick, 1960-

BX4668.A1 S88 2002
248.2′42′0922 — dc21   2002030456
[B]

06 07 08 09 10 9 8 7 6 5

Contents

Foreword

Deal Hudson

You have in your hands the stories of ten Catholic converts. None of them can possibly know your reasons for reading this volume. You may simply be curious, wondering why seemingly intelligent men and women would choose to join such a "backward" institution as the Catholic Church.

Isn't the Catholic Church the only institution in the world that opposes birth control and refuses to allow women into its leadership positions? Doesn't its clerical hierarchy, starting with the Pope and descending through its bishops, reflect a non-democratic and pre-modern view of authority?

And, on top of that, doesn't it rather foolishly expect its priests to live celibate lives?

The answer is yes. That's why those who enter the Church are often viewed with the same combination of amusement and derision reserved for people who insist that the earth is flat.

A convert, therefore, needs to have a sense of humor. He will inevitably become a target for remarks colored with unmistakable scorn, such as "How can you possibly have chosen to become a Catholic?" When I, a convert, hear this question asked in that tone of voice, I feel as if someone has asked me about my wife, "How could you possibly have married *her?*"

A convert quickly realizes that this kind of attitude is indigenous to the dominant culture. It's not really a secular culture, since a concern for "spirituality" is fairly pervasive, and Americans attend religious services at a higher percentage than any other country in the world. It would almost be preferable if people were honest enough to admit that they were secular, that they had excluded the supernatural from their religion and their daily lives. Instead, most people operate on the assumption that their own self-consciousness has an inviolate spiritual status against which nothing can make any claim.

Catholicism rejects this fundamental tenet of modern culture. To be a Catholic means your personal holiness, your "spirituality," is measured against the expectations of a transcendent God. Thus, in this culture, the Church must be a laughingstock.

There is something fundamentally anti-modern about becoming Catholic. This explains why a person who moves from, say, Presbyterianism to Catholicism is called a convert, while someone who moves from the Methodist Church to the Episcopalian is only changing denominations. Catholics are converts with a capital C because they reject a worldview that is taught through every media outlet in our culture. This worldview teaches that human beings are special because they have feelings, that the only wrong is hurting these feelings, and that good people should do all they can to promote enjoyment and pleasure in others. In short, the *summum bonum* of the present age is personal satisfaction — mental, emotional, and sexual.

When you choose to become Catholic, you can throw personal satisfaction out the window. Catholics constantly remind themselves of how they fall short of Christ's example of holiness. Consider the practice called penance. You're required to examine your sins regularly, thereby becoming intimate with your vices and habits of self-deception. What could be more countercultural than waking up each morning and asking yourself what you did wrong yesterday? Aren't we told that the key to self-esteem is to avoid such negative thoughts? A Catholic may feel relieved upon leaving the confessional, but he finds out quickly that holiness, not relief, is the point of Confession. The measure of holiness, a Catholic discovers, is not the satisfied mind, but life crucified and risen with Christ. When a Catholic is called to the Eucharist, he hears the words "Happy are those who are called to this Supper." He doesn't approach the Host expecting some miraculous infusion of New Age joy — a Catholic knows that happiness is intimately mingled with suffering, both the suffering of Christ and the suffering of those who bear His Cross.

Thus, Catholics are realists; they don't expect the members of the Body of Christ to be sinless. Catholics know and expect that priests and laity alike will fall short — sometimes well short — of an exemplary life. The sexual-abuse crisis in the Catholic Church is a case in point: Catholics, although disgusted and hurt by the crimes themselves, know that they cannot hold priests, who are sinful men themselves, to any higher or lower standard than they expect of any other person.

Because Catholics are realists, they are also a very forgiving people. Since acts of true penance lead to an experience of forgiveness, this dynamic of guilt and grace is situated at the heart of every practicing Catholic. Far from making converts regret their conversion, this scandal only reaffirms the importance of belonging to a Faith that can fully understand the reasons for such evils — and can lead evildoers to penance and forgiveness.

At times like these, converts sometimes find themselves in the awkward situation of encouraging cradle Catholics to hold on to the fundamentals of their Faith. Many Catholics who listen only to the mainstream media are led to believe that eliminating the tradition of priestly celibacy will solve the problem of sexual abuse in the priesthood.

Those who are born into the Faith have often not had the need or opportunity to think through the advantages of the Catholic tradition in the way a convert must. To the convert, the celibate priest stands as a magnificent example of what the Church teaches about the theology of the body: the priest in his celibacy attests to the same virtue of fidelity as do a faithful husband and wife. Taking celibacy away from the priesthood would send the clear message that the Church no longer believes in the ability of men and women to make a promise of fidelity and keep it.

These are problems that all Catholics must face, and ones that the convert feels in a special way. It would make sense in the eyes of the world to become a Catholic if it meant an increase in stature, wealth, or popularity; to become a Catholic while knowingly embracing the Church's brokenness and welcoming the world's scorn and ridicule seems almost unfathomable. These converts invite a great deal of hardship in their decision. But converts, even more so than cradle Catholics, find compensation in the fullness of joy and truth that transcends any temporal hardship. While others may be asleep to this reality, a convert's conscious choice is always with him, and the blessings of this choice are always in his mind.

Whether you are a Catholic or not, these stories will inspire you with their pursuit of truth in the face of all obstacles. I hope that they will encourage you in the same pursuit.

Introduction

Patrick Madrid

W hat a long, strange, and good trip it's been. Who could have predicted it?

In the fall of 1994, when I finished the first volume of the *Surprised by Truth* series, there was no way I could have foreseen the impact that book would have. At the time, the few people who seemed interested in books about converts could choose from several other such titles already on the market. The chances for commercial and apostolic success for yet another convert anthology — by an unknown, untested editor, published by a tiny, obscure new publishing house — seemed as remote as Pluto's orbit.

Eight years have passed. Today, with some three hundred thousand copies of the first volume alone in print (not to mention *Surprised by Truth 2*, which is steadily approaching one hundred thousand copies), it's immensely satisfying for me to introduce you to the third volume in this series.

As editor of and contributor to the *Surprised by Truth* books, I hope I can be forgiven for praising them, because what I'm praising are the people whose stories appear in them. They are the reason for the phenomenal success of these books. Their honest, unflinching (and sometimes even painful) examination of the reasons, divine and human, biblical and historical, for their conversions to the Catholic Church have proven remarkably able to reach past the barriers many people set up as a defense against the truth. Their stories have been for countless readers the instruments of grace that God has used to bring people home to Himself and to His Church. And for that (and for them) I thank the Lord with all my heart.

I'm doubly grateful to God for His allowing me to have had a hand in bringing these testimonies to a wide audience. As a cradle Catholic, I've always been humbled and amazed to find myself in the company of stalwart men and women who had to discover and choose what I was given at birth. I thank them all for their courage and conviction, which edify and fortify me in ways beyond description.

That, I think, is why the *Surprised by Truth* books are so effective: there's something inexplicably unique, something deeply powerful and penetrating, in these testimonies. Ultimately, of course, I attribute this potency to the Lord God Himself. It has been His grace, from start to finish, that has been active in the lives of each of these contributors and in the lives of those, like you, who read their stories.

And so, in that spirit of gratitude to God for His generous Providence expressed in and through the lives of so many converts to the Catholic Church, I'm very happy to share with you another group of wonderful men and women of deep faith and conviction.

In each chapter, you'll encounter a modern-day martyr — from the Greek word for "witness." By God's grace, these martyrs were willing to sacrifice anything to follow Him and to embrace His Truth. They are witnesses to the inexorable power and beauty of that Truth.

Surprised by Truth 3

A Twentieth-Century Centurion Swears Allegiance to Christ

From my Navy days fighting terrorism in the Middle East through my years debating politics at Oxford, Christ called me ever closer to His Church and finally into His priesthood.

Msgr. Stuart Swetland

June 14, 1985 began as a routine day at sea for me and the crew of the *U.S.S. Kidd*. Having just completed some joint naval exercises, we were in the Aegean Sea, en route to a port visit in Haifa, Israel. I was standing watch as the duty officer.

Suddenly the calm of the day was interrupted by reports that an American passenger plane, TWA Flight 847 out of Athens to Rome, had been hijacked to Beirut by two members of the radical terrorist group Islamic Jihad. On board were more than 150 passengers, mostly Americans — including five Navy divers. Petty Officer Second Class Robert Stethem would soon be tortured and shot in the head.

President Reagan planned to take decisive action. In less than forty-eight hours, we were off the coast of Beirut. Before long, other ships and special forces — including the then-secret Delta Force — began to join our growing flotilla.

My role was initially to serve as landing officer for the helicopters using our flight deck. But two hours before we were to launch, the captain summoned me into his cabin. He told me that a team of Navy SEALS was going to create a diversion ashore, drawing the enemy's fire before swimming out to sea. I was to command a small boat to pluck them from the water at high speed. The captain told me we would probably come under heavy fire and that the chance of casualties was greater than 50/50.

I chose the best unmarried men I could find for my three-man crew; then I prepared. I had been briefed on events in Beirut. I knew what the terrorists had done to Petty Officer Stethem. As I blackened my face with pitch and inspected the weapons we would load onto the boat, a great anger began to take hold of me. My anger gave way to hatred: hatred toward the cowardly thugs who had killed my shipmate. I was glad I had been chosen for this mission, even though it put my life in danger. I wanted to kill the terrorists who had killed Stethem.

We launched our operation at midnight, but almost immediately everything was put on hold. I found out later that President Reagan was waiting for further intelligence on the location of the hostages. He didn't want to leave any American behind. For the next two hours, we sat in the water, circling at our launch positions, waiting for the "go" command.

I pray the hate out of my heart

Then I did what I think every soldier, sailor, marine, or airman has done throughout history: I prayed. There are no atheists in foxholes. A recent convert to Catholicism, I had learned to pray the Rosary by reading the works of St. Louis Marie de Montfort,[1] and it had been the one form of prayer I had always

---

[1] St. Louis Marie de Montfort (1673-1716), secular priest who founded the Sisters of the Divine Wisdom and the Missionary

been able to use under any circumstances. It did not fail me that evening.

As I prayed, the words of the Our Father struck me as never before: "Forgive us our trespasses, as we forgive those who trespass against us." "Forgive?" How could God possibly ask me to forgive the bastards who had tortured and killed a brave American sailor?

My mind drifted to the sorrowful mysteries. Jesus being crucified: "Father, forgive them,"[2] He exclaimed as the nails pierced His sacred flesh. I thought of His admonition from the Sermon on the Mount: "Love your enemies."[3] How could God demand this? Surely this teaching had exceptions. As we circled in the choppy ocean waters off Beirut, I rediscovered what I already had come to know and believe: the gospel of Jesus Christ is true, and it does not admit of exceptions.

If I had died that night, my salvation would have been in jeopardy. I had hated those terrorists from my heart. I wanted them dead. I didn't just want to protect and free innocent hostages (a worthy effort where one can accept the death of an aggressor as an unintended consequence). I wanted to send the hijackers and their accomplices to Hell.

If I had died in that state, Hell is where I would have found myself.

But the "go" command never came. Before sunrise, President Reagan aborted the military operations, and negotiations eventually led to the release of the remaining hostages.

Priests of Mary and is known for his book *True Devotion to Mary*.

[2] Luke 23:34.

[3] Matt. 5:44.

Thanks be to God! For that night, floating in the darkness off the coast of Beirut, I had another conversion: I learned the meaning of mercy, forgiveness, and love. In those hours, God gave me the actual grace — the supernatural power — to help me let go of my hatred and wrath.

But I relied on another grace that night: the grace I had received in becoming Catholic. This grace allowed me to know and to believe in the truth of the teaching of Christ and His Church. In those moments before battle, if I had for a moment doubted that the Word of God as revealed in Scripture and Tradition was true, I believe I would have resisted God's call to "love your enemies," probably the most difficult command in Scripture. Without the faith to believe that the teaching of Christ and His Church are infallibly true, I would not have had the courage to change that evening.

God's grace not only saved me from myself that evening; this conversion from hatred to love — one of many in my life — brought me closer to discovering my call to the priesthood.

"Why did *you* become Catholic?"

The day that I was received into full communion with the Catholic Church was the most joyful day of my life. At the Easter Vigil in 1984, in the small chapel of Oxford University's Newman Center, I was confirmed and received the Eucharist for the first time. The moment I received the Host, I knew that I was being united with Jesus Christ in every possible way: physically, spiritually, emotionally, and intellectually. I knew that I was following the will of the Father more closely than I ever had before.

But becoming Catholic was about the last thing I had expected to do while at Oxford.

Often when someone asks, "Why did you become Catholic?" I answer with a clever line stolen from some famous convert. A favorite is G. K. Chesterton's quip "To get my sins forgiven." Another favorite is the short affirmation "Because it's true."

Sometimes it's more an accusation than a question. If the person asks, "Why did you become a *Catholic?*" with the emphasis on *Catholic*, he has a problem with the Church. If the emphasis is on *you*, he's usually an intellectual elitist who believes that no educated person would become (or remain) Catholic. If the emphasis is on *become*, the questioner finds it possible that a person raised in the Church would remain in it, but inconceivable that someone with my background would choose to *become* Catholic.

I love to challenge such prejudices, because I, too, once held them. When I "went up" to Oxford, as the English say (the expression assumes that everyone is coming from London, thus going "up," north, to Oxford) my religion could have best been described as lapsed Protestant with strong anti-Catholic biases. In many ways, I was a functioning pagan steeped in all the fashionable ideas of modern American ideology. Politically and economically, I was a conservative with a libertarian tendency. I was a pretty typical product of my background.

A born-again conservative in revolutionary times

I was born on May 15, 1959 in Pittsburgh, Pennsylvania, the youngest of three children. My parents were and are devout Christians, and I was baptized a Lutheran soon after birth. When I was three, my parents moved to rural northeast

7

Pennsylvania. There wasn't always a Lutheran church close at hand in those parts, so for the next decade, I attended Methodist and Baptist churches as well — each Evangelical, with a strong sense that the Bible was literally and inerrantly true. My family attended church every Sunday morning, participated in Sunday school (where my parents often assisted or taught), frequently attended midweek services on Wednesday nights, and encouraged prayer and Bible study at home.

At the age of six or seven, I committed myself to a personal relationship with Christ, as much as one can as a small child. I deepened this commitment at twelve, when, as a member of a Baptist community, I was "re-baptized." A few years later, when a Lutheran community began in our small town, I again recommitted myself when I was "confirmed" as a member there.

On each of these occasions, I was truly converting in the sense of going deeper into my relationship with Christ. I was really "growing in the Lord," a process that I believe parallels our Lord's own growth in "age and grace and wisdom."[4] This ongoing conversation is a necessary part of spiritual maturity.

But there was something missing. As I grew spiritually, I began to question many things. From my earliest memories, I have always been fascinated with moral questions, especially those that touch on economic and political issues. Perhaps this is because I grew up during the revolutionary times of the late 1960s and early 1970s in a house with a politically active, conservative Republican father. (My earliest political memory is of my dad's bumper sticker in 1966: "Don't blame me. I voted for Goldwater.") My elder siblings and my dad argued

---

[4] Cf. Luke 2:52.

constantly about Vietnam, the draft, the voting age, women's rights, civil rights, and a host of other issues.

Looking for the right answers

It was natural for me to search for answers to the questions that were being argued daily on television, in the newspaper, and at our dinner table. Having been taught to search for the truth in the Bible, I began to study it to find out the "right answers."

Even in my late teenage years, I questioned what seemed to be contradictory answers to the most basic questions from people who all claimed that God loves us and had given us the truth in Scripture. My mother and sister were working hard for women's rights because they saw the biblical truth that all people were created in the image and likeness of God and thus deserved equal respect. As an educator and administrator, my mother was a pioneer for women in leadership roles, although she never received the same pay as her (often less-qualified) male counterparts. But many Evangelicals condemned her and others like her for failing to be "submissive" according to their reading of St. Paul's epistles. Devout Christians read the same texts and came up with opposite conclusions!

On many issues, from the sublime (the meaning of Holy Communion) to the ridiculous (whether men could wear their hair long), I found believing Christians at odds, despite their reliance on the same Bible. Who was to decide among them? How could I decide what was right?

From the Naval Academy to a "peace church"

If I had stayed in my rural hamlet, these issues might never have been enough to cause me a crisis of faith. But the larger world beckoned. Partly because I wanted to get a free, high-quality education, partly because my parents had instilled in me the important notion of service, and partly for the prestige of it all, I entered the United States Naval Academy (USNA) as part of the class of 1981. Those in the admissions office informed my parents that they did not think I could handle the academy academically and not to expect much.

Born stubborn, I needed to hear no more. I threw myself into my studies (majoring in physics) and graduated first in my class, winning a Rhodes Scholarship in my senior year.

But my time at USNA was not good for my faith. During my plebe (freshman) year, I searched for a place to worship. The naval chaplaincy provided a generic Protestant service that I enjoyed but didn't find comforting or challenging. I began to look for a "civilian" church to attend. I was in for a shock. When I attended a Lutheran church in the Annapolis area, I was greeted coldly. After a couple of weeks, they told me I wasn't welcome back if I was in uniform — that they were a "peace church" that had taken an anti-war stance during the Vietnam conflict. Since plebes had to wear their uniforms, I couldn't attend this church.

This rejection left me reeling. My home community had celebrated my military scholarship and sent me forth with a blessing — and here were members of the same denomination, reading the same Bible, condemning me for being in the service. Who was right? How could I know?

The crucible of doubt

Being a typical eighteen-year-old, this was all I needed to quit practicing my faith. For the next four years, I was, at best, an irregular churchgoer. I stopped praying, and instead I threw myself into my work and studies. I did not resolve these faith issues; I just bracketed them, dismissing Christianity as a religion that was hopelessly confused.

When I arrived in Oxford in October 1981, I had an opportunity to study beyond my technological background. Former Rhodes Scholars from the Navy, including Admiral Stansfield Turner and Secretary of the Navy James Woolsey, had convinced me to study P.P.E. (politics, philosophy, and economics) at Oxford. I decided that this was a time to search for answers to the ethical and moral questions that had always interested me. In fact, my tutors at Oxford challenged me to do just that.

One of the first books they had me read was René Descartes' *A Discourse on Method* and his *Meditations on the First Philosophy* and *Principles of Philosophy*. Descartes challenges the reader to place all of his beliefs in the "crucible of doubt." This methodological doubt means that one should question why he holds any and all beliefs, even belief in the existence of God, in creation, and in himself. Through this method, Descartes reaches his famous *"Cogito ergo sum"* — "I think, therefore I am" — as the basis for a philosophical argument for the existence of God and the universe. I set about applying this method in my life.

Radical doubt is dangerous. By rejecting all received wisdom and tradition, you place yourself in an intellectual void. Only later would I understand that we are not isolated atoms, but, rather, beings born for and in community. We need to remain connected to that communion with the living and the dead and with the wisdom of the ages. As Chesterton said, "Belief in tradition is just applying the principles of democracy to the dead."

I confront Christianity's claims

Having begun to ask myself (and others) to justify all beliefs — moral, intellectual, and religious — I soon found myself face-to-face with the basic claims of Christianity. I could
no longer simply bracket them.

There God's grace worked in me, especially through certain Christians He placed in my life. As I began my studies at
New College in Oxford, a group of young men and women,
several of them believing Catholics, befriended me. During
our next three years together, their influence, patience, and
especially the witness of their lives helped lead me into the
Church.

Having inherited all the anti-Catholic prejudice of a typical Evangelical, I resisted what was becoming plain to me —
that there is a wisdom in the teaching of the Catholic Church
that is explainable only by its greater-than-human inspiration. As I searched for answers to the questions my tutors
asked me, I kept finding that the best — the most reasonable,
well-articulated, and convincing — responses came from the
Catholic Tradition. The writings of the saints (especially St.
Augustine and St. Thomas Aquinas, and those influenced by
them, such as John Henry Newman, Elizabeth Anscombe, and
John Finnis[5]) were superior to those proposed by other sources.
It seemed to me that Catholic thought about social questions — for example, the issues of war and peace (especially

[5] St. Augustine (354-430), Bishop of Hippo; St. Thomas Aquinas (c. 1225-1274), Dominican philospher, theologian, and
Doctor; John Henry Cardinal Newman (1801-1890), Catholic convert from the Anglican Church; Elizabeth Anscombe
(1919-2001), English philospher; John Finnis, Professor of
Law and Legal Philosophy, University College, Oxford.

the just-war tradition) — was clearer and better thought-out than other arguments that I was studying. At first I thought this was a coincidence; as time went on, I could not deny that something different was behind the writings of these men and women.

On my own, I began to examine the basic assumptions of the Christian Faith. First, did Jesus exist? Yes, this is well-documented. Next, is He who He says He is? I must admit that I agreed with C. S. Lewis's ideas that He was either "liar, lunatic, or Lord."[6] But how could I judge the authority of His claims?

The key question: did Jesus really rise?

After much thought and study (and just a little prayer — at this stage I wasn't yet seriously praying), I decided that the central claim of Christianity is the claim of Jesus' bodily Resurrection. The truth of the biblical witness seemed to me to hinge on this claim. So how should one judge the authenticity of the Resurrection?

I tried to approach the biblical texts like other ancient texts. At this time, I was also reading Julius Caesar and Thucydides for their insights into military strategy and tactics. Most thinkers accepted these texts fairly straightforwardly. Was Scripture less trustworthy?

The text I first found most compelling was 1 Corinthians 15. Here St. Paul tells of all those who had seen and experienced the risen Lord: more than five hundred witnesses, many

---

[6] Jesus could have been only one of three things: a liar who deceived His followers; a lunatic who was deluded about His own identity; or who He said He was: the divine Lord and Messiah.

of whom were still alive when Paul wrote the letter (about twenty years after the events). This letter seems to be an authentic testimony to the truth of the bodily Resurrection of Jesus. The hundreds of witnesses lend credibility to Paul's own experience of the risen Lord. If these others had not really experienced the convincing proofs of Jesus' Resurrection,[7] Paul would quickly have been seen as a fraud.

As I studied more, I was startled by the overwhelming evidence for the Resurrection, especially in the life of the early Church. Almost to a person, those first believers went to a martyr's death for their firm and certain belief in the Resurrection. No other explanation made sense of the data. That Jesus really had not died? No, the medical evidence in John's Gospel of "blood and water gushing forth from His side"[8] shows that He really died. Plus, even a cursory reading of Roman history shows that no Roman soldier would so botch a crucifixion as to allow a condemned man to survive.

No, for anyone "with eyes to see and ears to hear,"[9] the accounts of the Resurrection and the lives of the men and women who had witnessed the life, death, and Resurrection of Jesus were convincing evidence of the authenticity of the Resurrection.

The Church's teachings all ring true

In addition, there were existential, subjective reasons for me to believe. Throughout my sojourn away from practicing Christianity, I had never been comfortable in denying what I

[7] Cf. Acts 1:3.
[8] Cf. John 19:34.
[9] Cf. Matt. 13:16.

had experienced in prayer and worship as a child. On some level of my being, I knew that I had encountered the living God in my life. I could not "unhear" that Word that had spoken to my heart as a child. Now my mind was united with what I knew connaturally in my heart all along: that Jesus is our risen Lord!

With this rediscovery, I began studying the Scriptures closely, looking for a community of believers in which to worship. I found one in an Evangelical Anglican Church in Oxford. But after a few months of worshiping there, I found I needed more than just that wonderful community's charismatic preaching and singing.

I now *really* knew, on an adult level, that the Scriptures were true. I wanted to find a community that also believed this and was trying to live it daily. I also wanted to answer the many ethical, moral, and political questions that still intrigued me.

As I studied and prayed more, I kept encountering the issues that divided Catholics and Evangelical Protestants. I read of how Jesus had commissioned His Apostles to forgive sin in John 20:22-23,[10] but where and how was this power exercised today in the community? Scripture talked about anointing the sick in James 5:14-15,[11] yet only Catholics seemed to take

---

[10] "And when He had said this, He breathed on them and said to them, 'Receive the Holy Spirit. If you forgive the sins of any, they are forgiven; if you retain the sins of any, they are retained.' "

[11] "Is any among you sick? Let him call for the elders of the church, and let them pray over him, anointing him with oil in the name of the Lord; and the prayer of faith will save the sick man, and the Lord will raise him up; and if he has committed sins, they will be forgiven."

this text seriously. What Jesus said about Holy Communion seemed very straightforward to me, especially in John 6, yet Evangelicals speak of the Lord's Supper as only symbolic. The scriptures talked about the transformative power of God's grace, so that one can speak like St. Paul of total transformation of oneself to become "another Christ,"[12] but Evangelicals believe that Christ's righteousness merely covers our sinful nature instead of transforming it. Sacred Scripture speaks of the intercession of the heavenly host on behalf of God's people on earth,[13] but only Catholics prayed to the saints and angels as intercessors and friends.

Then there was the moral teaching of the Church, which seemed to make more sense to me each day. As I examined the alternatives, secular and religious, no other ethical system had the same internal consistency and tight argumentation that I found in the Catholic moral tradition of natural law. In addition, the Catholic moral tradition answered the question of *how to decide* moral issues — by appealing to the teaching authority given to the Apostles and to their successors (the Magisterium of the Church). This teaching authority made sense of God's love and desire to lead His children into all truth.

Still another influence was the example of the Catholics I knew as friends, who lived their Faith with a peace and joy about them that I didn't find elsewhere in the world. In fact, it was a peace and joy that "surpassed all understanding."[14] I knew that I needed and desired that same peace and joy.

[12] Cf. Gal. 2:19-20.
[13] Cf. Rev. 8.
[14] Cf. Phil. 4:7.

I sense the Real Presence

I began seeking private instruction in the Faith from Oxford's Catholic chaplain. For two and a half years, he patiently met with me each week as I struggled to learn what the Catholic Church teaches. I examined every aspect of the Faith that I could handle. I attended lectures on questions of Faith and morals held around the university. I visited with Fr. Thomas More Mann, a saintly Franciscan who introduced me to a side of the Church entirely new to me: its outreach to the poor and vulnerable. I began to pray seriously and to attend Mass each day. I loved to pray before and after Mass in the chapel in front of the tabernacle.

Growing up, I had been exposed to different theologies of the Eucharist. To the Baptists and Methodists, it was only a symbolic remembrance. Lutherans believed in "consubstantiation": Jesus is present "with" (*con*) the substance of bread and wine, but only in its "use" as communion. The elements remained bread and wine at all times. In fact, I once watched my Lutheran pastor return extra communion hosts to the bag for a later use after they had been consecrated. When I questioned him about this practice, he told me that they were no longer consecrated because Jesus was present only in the "use." When I pressed him for how this was possible and how this squared with Jesus' own words "This *is* my Body; this *is* my Blood," he told me that it was a mystery that we couldn't hope to understand.

As I prayed in that chapel day in and day out, I had a very real sense of Jesus' abiding presence in that place. When I finally got to the Church's teaching on the Eucharist, I grew excited: I had been experiencing the Real Presence in my own private prayer in the chapel.

The Church is a truth-teaching thing

Once I became conceptually aware of what I had connaturally experienced with the Eucharist, I began truly to hunger and thirst for our eucharistic Lord. But before I could receive Him, I had to be honestly able to say that I believed what the Catholic Church believed. So I redoubled my efforts to study the teachings of the Church, trying to come to terms with them, particularly her sexual ethic, which seemed so idealistic; it was beautiful but seemed impossibly demanding.

By this time, my friends knew I was examining questions of the Faith. I was trying to see whether I could accept every aspect of the Church's teaching. But my friend Dermot Quinn pointed out to me the futility of this approach. Even if I could study every detail of every teaching and come to say honestly that I agreed with the Church, this would not make my faith truly Catholic. What made a person Catholic, Dermot insisted, was not just belief that the Church taught the truth in matters of Faith and morals, but the belief that the Church is a "truth-teaching thing." In other words, the most important question I had to answer was "Is the Catholic Church who she says she is?" Is she the Church founded by Jesus Christ, containing all that Christ's believers need for their instruction and sanctification?

If I believed this, I should be (had to be!) Catholic. If I did not, it really didn't matter whether I happened to agree with particular Church teachings.

The choice before me was clear. I *had* come to believe that the Church was who she claimed to be. The fact that I still had difficulties with some of her teachings didn't really matter. As Newman said, "A thousand difficulties do not make for one doubt." I didn't doubt that the Church was the Mystical Body of Christ extended through space and time. I was confident that the Church's teachings in Faith and morals were true even if I didn't fully understand why they were true, because I believed that God had endowed His Church with a special charism of the Holy Spirit that ensured that her authentic teachings in matters of Faith and morals are, at least, not false. So I was ready to be received into full communion.

I knew then, as I know now, that my life as a Catholic would partly be spent in coming to a better understanding of my Faith. I would need to do theology ("faith seeking understanding") to know and live the truth better.

This point needs to be emphasized: If God truly loves us, then He must ensure that we have a way of knowing what He is like and how we are to live. A loving father wants to be known by his children and teaches his children how to live and how to love. Any father who didn't would be negligent. I had come to know and experience that our loving Abba is no "reclusive" father. He has provided us, His children, with a way to know how we should live. The teaching office of the Church ensures that in every age we have access to the fullness of truth that has been revealed to us in Jesus Christ, who empowers the Church's official teachers, the bishops in union with the Bishop of Rome, to teach with a greater-than-human authority in the areas of Faith and morals. He does this out of love for His children. But, like all children, we must attentively listen to our Father and seek to understand His teachings if we are to live them out.

It is also very important for us to have confidence and trust in this function of the Magisterium of the Church. This is especially true when it comes to accepting *and living* the difficult and demanding teachings of the gospel. When faced with temptation, often coupled with intense emotions, we have a tendency toward rationalization. In such difficult times, we must have at least moral certitude about the teaching authority of the Church. One of the great injustices that dissenting theologians, pastors, and teachers have done to God's people is to place uncertainty in people's minds, doubts about Church teachings and even about the very authority of the Church to teach. This makes it easier for us to use our difficulties and doubts as excuses not to live up to the demands of the gospel.

Answering the call planted in my heart

That June night in 1985 off the coast of Beirut, I needed certainty that God did in fact demand that I love my enemies. I needed confidence that God's promises to me would be fulfilled. I needed to know that God's grace was sufficient for me to follow the gospel's call to love. Without this confidence, I could well have lost my soul.

Once received into the Church, I was soon back in the Navy, serving as a line officer aboard frigates and destroyers. I found it challenging to try to live as a devout Catholic in the military. It was particularly difficult not to be able to attend daily Mass. At sea, we would often go two months without seeing a Catholic chaplain or making a port visit. But I was determined to serve the Lord as I served my country. It was the height of the Cold War, and it was easy to see that the Soviets and their empire needed to be contained. As I was soon to learn firsthand, innocents needed protection throughout the world, especially from the threat of terrorism that was (and is) affecting so many.

Throughout my time of service, but especially after the events of the summer of 1985, an old desire began to re-emerge in my soul. When I was five or six, if you had asked me what I wanted to be when I grew up, I would have said a minister. Of course, I had put away such "childish thoughts"[15] as I grew, especially in light of my struggle with faith. But now they began to re-emerge. I discussed these feelings with spiritual advisers, who recommended that I wait three years after my conversion before acting on them. Converts often can be overly zealous when it comes to their desire to serve the Lord.

I loved the Navy. But over time, I became more and more convinced that God was calling me to a higher form of service: the priesthood. I wanted to share with others the joy I had experienced — the joy of knowing God's forgiveness, the joy of receiving Him in the Eucharist, and the joy of knowing the truth revealed to us in His Word. I resigned my commission in order to enter the seminary, was ordained a priest on May 25, 1991, and have had the honor to serve most of my priesthood as a Newman Center chaplain.

As a "Newman convert" myself, I feel right at home in this capacity. Each day God challenges me to go deeper into the mystery of His love. In hindsight, I see my life as a constant call to just such an ongoing conversion. At times I'm faithful to this call, and other times I fall far short of a proper response to His grace. What has been true all through my life is that the Lord continues to be "kind and merciful to me, a sinner."[16] My greatest joy as a priest is sharing that kindness and mercy with others — even with my enemies.

[15] Cf. 1 Cor. 13:11.
[16] Cf. Luke 18:13.

I Succumb to Roman Fever

For years I resisted the siren song of Catholicism.
When finally I left the Anglican Church for Rome,
I died to my old life, but found a life more abundant.

David Mills

What beauty was once ours," I said to my wife as we drove along the coast north of Boston, looking over the waving salt marsh grasses to the ocean just beyond and the blue sky stretching above. My wife and I had lived for thirteen years on this coast, first in Beverly and then in the small town of Ipswich (said to be the real setting of John Updike's novel *Couples*) before I was called to serve at an Episcopal seminary outside Pittsburgh, which was for me well into the Midwest.

Driving around our old home, we felt a deep, almost painful sense of homesickness. I had loved the salt marshes especially, but almost everything I saw made my heart ache: the clapboard houses, the old barns, the slightly rolling fields, the stone walls running through the woods, the old stone library where my wife had worked, the stream where our firstborn had fed the ducks, even the little seafood restaurant shaped like the paper box they give you to take home your clams.

We felt that, living near Pittsburgh, we weren't where we should be. We were estranged from something that should have been ours. The feeling passed, of course — we had a home to go back to, and friends, a job, and a church — but it will return just as strongly the next time we visit.

Almost everyone has felt this longing to be home (a close friend of mine even feels it for southern California). It is the closest experience I know to that longing for the Catholic Church that Anglicans call "Roman Fever." When you suffer this fever, you feel as if you are living in exile and as if you can't be happy until you go home. You feel a great, aching desire to be a Catholic.

A yearning that comes and goes

Roman Fever was, at least for me, much like malaria. It comes and goes unexpectedly. When you have it, you feel as if it's going to take you off to Rome (a sort of death for the Anglo-Catholic), but when you get better, you easily forget it. When you don't have it, you tend to think of it as a chronic illness to be suffered until it goes away and you can get back to doing what you think you're supposed to be doing.

I'd get the fever most often when reading the works of Catholic writers, although it sometimes came apparently un-provoked. J. R. R. Tolkien's *Lord of the Rings*, Evelyn Waugh's later novels, Flannery O'Connor's letters, Graham Greene's "Catholic novels," and almost any of G. K. Chesterton's books could set it off. Sigrid Undset's *Kristin Lavransdatter* could bring it on, as could Walker Percy's essays and Ronald Knox's apologetics. I loved John Henry Newman — he's my hero — but I knew that if I read him, I'd feel this painful, aching desire to do what he had done.

I could get the fever from reading writers who didn't be-lieve in Catholicism and even from writers who hated it. I had read Albert Camus' books from early adolescence, and they had sometimes led me to look wistfully at the Catholic Church long before I had the slightest interest in joining her, perhaps because the faith he didn't believe in was the Catholic Faith. Several of the most honest and acute analysts of the modern world had the same effect. George Orwell hated the Catholic Church, but almost everything he wrote showed me that she alone was the answer to the questions he (and I) asked.

At times, I carefully avoided anything that might bring on Roman Fever. I would leave Chesterton's books on the shelf and busy myself with something else. I didn't want to feel so strongly an urge to do what I didn't want to do, and I'm not sure, now, whether I was sinning against the light. Like malaria, it kept coming anyway, until one day I realized that if I kept refusing the invitation, it might not come again.

I had known several Anglicans, most of them priests, who told me about their own youthful Roman Fever and assured me that it would eventually go away. They looked back on it as you look back on your twelve-year-old passion for baseball cards or the earnest discussions of ultimate questions you had with friends in your dorm room late at night. I was an Anglican then, and active in Anglican affairs, but I always felt that they had done something wrong, even though I thought, or tried to convince myself I thought, that they had done the right thing in rejecting a distraction from their ministry.

The malarial kind of Roman Fever may be simply the Anglican form. The Roman Fever most Evangelicals suffer doesn't come and go, but once contracted, only grows worse: it keeps them sweating through sleepless nights, feeling themselves to be out of their senses. They suffer for years without a break until it finally carries them off or they harden their hearts and cure themselves once for all.

The Anglo-Catholic panacea

I suspect Anglicans suffer the malarial type because modern Anglicanism can look so much like Catholicism. In some forms, it looks and feels and sounds Catholic, and it lets you feel Catholic even when you aren't. You have vestments and Liturgy and a sacramental life; you have some idea of tradition and some belief in the Anglican Church as a living body going back through its bishops to the Lord Himself; you have saintly examples of devotion and theologians of weight. It is mostly a charade, of course, but it inoculates you against the real appeal of the Catholic Church, as a dose of cowpox keeps you from getting smallpox. It is Catholicism Lite.

But this is so only in the versions usually called "high church" or "Anglo-Catholic." The Anglo-Catholic claims to be fully Catholic without what he would tactfully call "the Roman additions." His is the Faith of the primitive Church, and Roman Catholicism the Faith of the late medieval Church (a sort of code for "corrupt"), to which have been added a few unfortunate developments, such as the declaration of papal infallibility. The Anglo-Catholic's is a cleaner, sparer, truer Catholicism.

He explains the Protestant origin of his own church, and the decisive Protestantism of its doctrinal statements, by saying that the Reformers naturally went too far in trying to purify the Catholic Church. They threw out the baby with the bath water; the Anglo-Catholic claims to have rescued the baby, leaving Rome (by implication) with the dirty bath water.

He has also to explain how he could be Catholic and hold to his church's Protestant statements at the same time. The Anglo-Catholic might love Benediction and Corpus Christi processions, but he has in Anglicanism's *Articles of Religion* — its constitution — the order that "The sacraments were not ordained of Christ to be gazed upon, or to be carried about," which seems to rule out Benediction and Corpus Christi processions without appeal. He solves this problem by claiming that of course the *Articles* are correct, but as long as the sacrament is used properly, for the purposes for which Christ ordained it, it can also be gazed upon and carried about in full obedience to the *Articles*. This isn't an honest reading of his founding documents, whose authors meant to ban Benediction and Corpus Christi outright, but it's the sort of thing one has to do to be a Catholic in a Protestant Church.

Some Anglo-Catholics tried to get around this problem by claiming that the Reformation documents didn't bind them. They appealed to an "English Catholicism" that began before the Reformation and whose cause they championed even though the religious body of which they were a part was still controlled by Protestants and governed by Protestant documents. American Episcopalians would argue that the *Articles of Religion* weren't an authority for Episcopalians, even though they lived in full communion with the Church of England, for which the *Articles* were still the doctrinal standard. Even when I was most convinced of Anglicanism, I always felt that this was all special pleading and wouldn't stand up.

But however he tries to settle the problem of trying to be a Catholic in a Protestant Church, the Anglo-Catholic is committed by his theology to the idea that he's more Catholic than the Pope. The Pope believes things (so the Anglo-Catholic thinks) that aren't true, not least the claim that a Christian ought to be in communion with him, and that the life and faith of Christians who aren't in full communion with the

Holy See (including the Anglo-Catholic) are somehow defec-
tive. The Pope, the Anglo-Catholic asserts, is in error on these
and several other substantial matters.

Anglo-Catholics of 100 and 150 years ago would say this,
but most modern Anglo-Catholics can't bring themselves to
say it unless pressed very hard. They can't escape the reality of
the Catholic Church, which makes such claims look foolish.
Their grandfathers had lived in a much smaller and more self-
protective world, in which the Catholic Church in England or
America could be dismissed as "the Italian mission." They
have before them the Catholic Church in her size and range,
the witness of her popes, her intellectual breadth and sub-
tlety, and her doctrinal coherence. Faced with the Catholic
Church, they naturally avoid saying aloud, "We are the truer
Catholics."

This is a hard way to live, being committed by your position to the belief that yours was the true Catholicism, but
knowing how absurd this sounds even to yourself. Perhaps that
is the reason Anglicans suffer from the malarial form of Roman Fever, as first one side and then the other takes control.

All may, some should, none must

It is the style, I know, for converts to say how much they
loved their old churches and how much they learned from
them. I'm sure this is true for me, but, a year after becoming a
Catholic, I feel that Anglicanism's main effect on my life was
to help me avoid becoming a Catholic. Anglicanism allowed
me to suffer Roman Fever without seeking the obvious cure.

I look back at my life as an Anglo-Catholic and marvel at the
degree of self-deception it required. I called myself a Catholic,
but I made up my Catholicism, taking what bits and pieces I

I Succumb to Roman Fever

thought genuine and rejecting the rest. My fellow Anglo-Catholics did the same. You might believe in the Assumption, or you might not, but the matter was left to you. If you believed it, you would probably call it "a matter of personal devotion" and be perfectly happy with a fellow Anglo-Catholic who rejected it because he didn't find it taught explicitly in Scripture or the early Church.

The same held true for moral doctrines and spiritual disciplines. Most Anglo-Catholics I knew thought contraception a good thing, and many of them thought the Catholic marital discipline "rigid" and "unpastoral." The standard rule for confession was "All may, some should, none must." What constituted Catholic discipline was to a great extent up to you, and your Catholicism might differ from your priest's or your neighbor's, depending on what you found "helpful."

The Anglo-Catholic asserts his Catholicism as a personal choice, against the body in which he lived. His church was founded as a Protestant church, and all its documents were Protestant documents, and the great majority of its members were Protestants by conviction, but he claims to be as Catholic a Christian as his Roman Catholic neighbor solely because he believes something he calls the Catholic Faith.

When away from home, the Anglo-Catholic happily takes communion from an Anglican pastor who believes that the bread he holds is only bread, but in his own parish, he believes that his priest, who was ordained in the same church as that pastor, who had been given the same authority as he (and perhaps by the same bishop), holds the Body of Christ.

It was a world with many godly people doing godly work, who were, as far as I know, as sincere in their devotion as any Christian, but it wasn't the Catholic Church.

I always knew this, I think, although I would repress the obvious questions when they came to mind. Perhaps having a bad conscience about claiming to be a Catholic leaves you vulnerable to Roman Fever.

Playing chicken with the Church

Someone who knows more about converts will have to decide how many people suffer this form of Roman Fever. My story, which is that of many other Anglicans I know, is a different story from the ones many converts can tell.

They were dragged into the Church with their arms flailing and their heels dug in, while, for more than twenty years, I walked quite happily at the edge of the Church, occasionally looking in a door or window, but mostly living happily outside and telling myself that the outside was as good, and in some ways better, than the inside. My Roman Fever was, of course, a good thing, in that it reminded me that I wasn't where I ought to be, but it was also a bad thing, in that I knew I had only to wait it out and then I could go back to my life without having to change anything.

And in a perverse sort of way, which I can't explain, my Roman Fever made me think I didn't have to do anything else and made me feel slightly superior to my poor Protestant friends who never had it. Many of us felt we were doing something dangerous, something rather daring, by playing chicken with the Catholic Church. I feel embarrassed by it now, but it felt serious at the time.

The Anglican who suffers from Roman Fever doesn't struggle with Catholic claims, as his Evangelical brethren do. Whereas the Evangelical finds the path to Rome covered with stumbling blocks, the Anglican finds it smooth. He will often think (I certainly did) that the Evangelical is stumbling over pebbles.

I knew saintly Evangelicals who were horrified by the idea of liturgical worship, but also horrified by how much they liked it. They would trot out, with an urgency that betrayed a guilty conscience, all the usual arguments: mainly that such services were insincere and bound the Spirit in human forms. They were quite insistent that a formal and regular service was a bad thing.

I had spent enough time in Protestant churches to know that Protestant worship was as liturgical as anyone else's. Move the prayers in a Baptist service, and half the congregation will revolt — and not from mere conservatism, either. The prayers, they would say, are there for a reason. The service has a logic to it. There are reasons that it begins with a hymn and that the Bible readings come before the sermon. I have been told that Pentecostal services are equally formal, in the sense of having a regular and predictable form. The Holy Spirit is allowed to move at certain times but not others. One had best not interrupt the sermon with a "word of knowledge."

Given this, I never understood why written liturgies upset my Evangelical friends, unless they disliked them simply because they were "Catholic" and therefore bad. I thought that the Catholic Church worshiped liturgically because people were liturgical creatures. This wasn't, as people say, rocket science.

Neither saints nor sinners scandalize me

My Evangelical friends were even more horrified by the idea of saints: not just by the idea of praying to the saints, but of having anyone set off from the rest of us as a superior kind of

Christian. Once, shortly after I had discovered the Episcopal Church, two very sweet little old ladies, hearing me refer to St. Paul, gently reprimanded me by saying, "We're saints, too." The only answer, which I didn't make, having been taught to respect my elders, was "No, you're not." It struck me then — I was a barely Christianized high school student — that they were presuming a status they didn't have and hadn't earned.

The same Evangelicals lived on biographies of great Protestant heroes, especially missionaries. Their magazines were filled with stories of great men and women doing great things for God. If anything, they tended to hero-worship. Yet they would sometimes get quite angry to hear anyone from the past called "saint." They gave Mary no special place in their systems and, when they did mention her, put her far down the list of Evangelical heroes, behind Hudson Taylor and Billy Graham and any Christians among the NFL's active quarterbacks.

Nor was I bothered by the scandals Evangelicals described with horror. Having grown up in a New England college town, and having absorbed in high school what was then called "humanistic Marxism," I had some sense of history and thought it obvious that an institution as old and as big as the Catholic Church would be full of bad members and good members who made bad mistakes.

When one of the Church's critics would shriek "Galileo!" I would answer, "Yes. *And* . . . ?" They thought the mistreatment of Galileo (to the extent he was mistreated) proved that the Church was so ignorant and repressive that you couldn't trust her. I thought it only showed that the Church was a human institution of her time, which everybody already knew. It did not suggest an answer to the question of whether that human institution was also divine.

My Evangelical friends thought that because important Catholics had lied or murdered or slandered or cheated, had made black people sit at the back of the church, had preached celibacy while having mistresses, or had committed some horrifying crime in the name of the Church, the Church was a sham. I thought the stories yet more evidence that God works in mysterious ways. Once you admit that God has given His authority to fallen men, as the Evangelicals themselves did, you had to expect the scandals.

What moved me, however, was finding, among all the horrors that sinful Catholics had committed, sign after sign of sanctity, which couldn't be explained except as the special work of grace. There were Catholic Nazis, of course, but there were also Edith Stein and Franz Jaegerstaetter.[17] Rapacious Catholic businessmen cheated the poor, but Mother Teresa and Dorothy Day lived in poverty to serve them. Catholics in central Europe shot their neighbors, but Pope John Paul II forgave the man who shot him.

Even in high school, I always looked for the inexplicable signs of God's grace — the saints, the ordinary godly people, the Pope, the countercultural teaching, the wisdom — that rose like peaks over the smog of indifference and turpitude, and these I found in the Catholic Church in abundance. I was reassured by the fact that in the Church, the Fall does not have the last word, although every human consideration says

---

[17] St. Edith Stein (1891-1942), Jewish convert to the Catholic Faith who became a Carmelite nun and was martyred in Auschwitz; St. Franz Jaegerstaetter (1907-1942), Austrian who, on the day St. Edith Stein was killed at Auschwitz, was martyred by the Nazis for refusing to serve in the German military.

it should. There was something in it the sociologist and historian could not explain, which I took as a hint of the divine.

It seemed to me that the Evangelicals were winning the argument by sleight of hand. (Liberals and secularists did this as well.) A bad Catholic is still a Catholic, and every other Catholic is stuck with him; but an Evangelical simply disowns anyone in his crowd who goes bad, by claiming that he's no longer an Evangelical. (Some years later, when I got to know something of the inside of Evangelicalism, I found that Evangelicals in fact had no right to point fingers at the Catholic Church — and I wasn't even thinking then of their approval of contraception and remarriage after divorce, but only of the usual sexual and financial scandals.)

As I said, none of the things that bothered my Evangelical friends ever bothered me — not the Mass, not the invocation of the saints, not Purgatory, not the Pope, not indulgences. All of those things seemed true to me. I had a few questions about the Pope's universal jurisdiction, but even these were more academic than personal. Why, then, didn't I become a Catholic?

Why I nonetheless resisted Roman Fever

I can give four reasons, in descending order of defensibility: a genuine conviction that the church in which I lived was a Catholic one if not the fully Catholic one; a feeling that I had work to do where I was; the need to support my family; and sloth.

I could explain each of these at length, but I think most readers will understand them. I admit to having never felt entirely convinced of the first three, and I admit that the fourth was a much greater hindrance than I then realized. As a friend said about her family's move to the Catholic Church, "For eight years it was just a flirtation; the last two were serious courtship." It's embarrassing to have been a flirt and to have flirted with something as noble and dignified as the Catholic Church, but I must confess that I failed to be as serious as I ought to have been. Now I think, "How, oh how, could you have thought being an Episcopalian was worth not being a Catholic, when becoming a Catholic was so easy to do?"

Why I finally succumbed to it

In the end, two insights brought me over the line. The first was the simple realization that I had to make a choice, lest I harden my heart one too many times and never get Roman Fever again. I became a Catholic in part because one day I realized that God might stop giving me times when my heart and mind were so well allied that I could more easily overcome the inertia that kept me where I was. This insight was, as far as I can tell, the work of the Spirit.

If this first insight pulled me toward the Church, the second insight pushed me in. About a year before my wife and I began instruction, I sat for several days in a discussion about divorce and remarriage with twelve Evangelicals — all learned, all biblically conservative, all holding more or less the same hermeneutic — who came to nine different and, to some extent, deeply opposed positions.

At the end of all the reading and talk, they appealed to a shared ideal (lifelong marriage) and offered a range of views on the acceptable ways to fail to reach the ideal. What Anglicans had thought for centuries was the nature of marriage as taught in Scripture became for all but one of them only an ideal, and they disagreed only about how far from the ideal one could fall and still receive the Church's blessing.

Almost all argued that the Bible is unclear on the question of divorce and remarriage and that it can legitimately be read in different ways, at which point one has to ask, "What use is it, if it fails to teach clearly on this matter?" They thought God had left the issue open, the sole evidence for which was that they didn't agree with each other.

This diversity bothered me, but what bothered me more was that no one but me found it a problem. Here were learned and godly men who read the Bible the same way, but who couldn't agree on what it said about a matter crucial to the Church's life and to human happiness. Their belief in the supremacy of Scripture, their learning, and their great skill in reading Scripture didn't give them any real assurance that they knew what it taught.

I thought that God couldn't have meant us to live in such confusion and with such an effectively minimalistic doctrine — which had already grown and would grow ever more minimal as the members of the self-identified Evangelical party disagreed more and more. But this minimalism, I suddenly realized, was one of the principles of the church to which I belonged, as held by its finest servants. They would hold as authoritative only what they agreed Scripture said, and they were agreeing on less and less.

This, I realized, isn't the Catholic Church. I had known this for years, but only with the earnest discussion of my friends — showing that those with the highest view of the authority of Scripture couldn't tell you authoritatively what it said — did the insight become a reason to move. I could no longer convince myself that in being an Anglican I was a Catholic — if not a complete one, still enough of one to qualify.

I could no longer think of Roman Fever as an illness to be endured and began to see it as an invitation, because I knew that my heart had long seen so much more clearly than my mind what I ought to do. My friends' long conversation led me to see the sign that had been written in front of me in letters ten feet tall, which I had always managed to miss: the sign that told me the obvious: "If you want be a Catholic, you must be a Catholic."

The deeper reason

In explaining the seductions of Roman Fever, I don't want to give the wrong impression. It was a gift of grace, although it didn't feel like one at the time. I had it in the first place because I began to love the Catholic Church. I began to love her saints and great men such as John Paul II and Cardinal Ratzinger. I saw that she alone fought for the things I was fighting for, such as the lives of the unborn. I found in her leading minds a commitment to reason found nowhere else. And I found in her also a pastoral wisdom that understood human frailty without giving up the call to sanctity.

But in the end, I began to love the Catholic Church for the Mass, because in her my Lord and God came to me. My Roman Fever finally broke when I could no longer stay outside the place where God could be touched and tasted.

Sex, Lies, and the Catholic Church

Infidelity and selfishness threatened our picture-perfect
family, until we discovered the Church's life-giving
teachings about love and marriage.

An interview with Greg and Julie Alexander

JULIE: Our lives began to spin out of control when our
daughter was born.

She was our second child. While I was still in the hospital,
the doctor said, "You have such a perfect family! You have
your boy; you have your girl. How wonderful! Now one of you
needs to get fixed."

"What do you mean, 'fixed'?" we asked. We thought that
was something you did to dogs.

"Well, Greg can get a vasectomy or you can get a tubal."

We thought about it, and it seemed like a good idea. We
already had a great, beautiful family! Why not?

Greg decided that since I had had the children, he would
get the vasectomy. We were both Catholics, but we thought
there was nothing wrong with the idea. Two kids were enough.

That decision would nearly cost us our marriage. It devastated our children and weakened what little faith in God that
we had.

GREG: Yet God was merciful. We were sick. We were hurting. We were dead. But through Christ and through His

39

Catholic Church, through the beautiful sacraments we have, we were brought back to life.

JULIE: We were both brought up in the Church, but as children neither of us grasped the importance of the Faith. My parents were devout. Primarily they showed us their faith not in their words, but in their actions. As I grew up, I saw them as so holy that, in a sense, their example backfired: I thought it was just too hard to live that way. That was for them to do, not for me! My brothers and sister and I knew the *whats* of our Faith — we knew we had to go to church — but we didn't know *why*.

That's not because our parents didn't tell us. I just wasn't listening! I was living my Faith for my parents' sake, not for a personal relationship with God. I went to church because I knew they wanted me to. It was more out of habit and to keep up appearances than for any other reason.

GREG: I went through the motions and did the things I needed to do: First Communion, Confirmation. But I never really had a true understanding either, despite the fact that I was an altar server.

My grandfather was a Baptist minister. Many of my cousins are still Baptist ministers. Even today, I'm the only practicing Catholic in my family, although my dad has just recently come back.

When my parents converted to Catholicism, I was in third grade. I was awestruck the first time I went to Mass. I remember the statues, the Stations of the Cross, the icons, the candles. It was beautiful, and I was very excited by all of it. I remember the attraction of being an altar server. It was cool: kids processing up in white, carrying the cross. That was something that I wanted to do.

We did go to church a lot as a family, but through the years my parents stopped going as much. At a certain point, I went more than they did, because I usually served at the altar! I was familiar with the Church, comfortable with the Church, but I didn't understand the Faith.

Julie and I grew up the way most ordinary Americans do: we didn't think much about spiritual things. We wanted to find jobs that would make us some money and enable us to live comfortable lives.

We met in college in 1984, at St. Edward's University in Austin, Texas. St. Edward's was a Catholic university, but that had nothing to do with our choosing to go there. I was there only because I had a basketball scholarship!

Our life together begins in sin

JULIE: My parents were excited about St. Edward's because it was a Catholic school, but I chose it because I liked Austin. There was a church on campus, but our Faith wasn't a part of who we were. I went to Mass because I was afraid that my dad would find out that I wasn't going!

GREG: I felt obligated to go to Mass because I was dating Julie, not because I had a relationship with God.

On our first date, we both said that we'd like to spend the rest of our lives together! We enjoyed being around each other. We felt comfortable with each other. We felt the ability to be open and to communicate. But from the beginning, almost everything that we did was incompatible with the Faith. Premarital sex, living together, chasing after money and material things.

JULIE: I was doing what everyone else was doing, so I didn't think I was doing anything wrong. I certainly didn't know I

41

had to confess premarital sex or living together. I didn't think about the way we were living. Sure, I felt a twinge, deep down, that something was wrong. But I thought it was just feelings of guilt left over from my upbringing.

I know now it was the Holy Spirit speaking to my conscience. But there was nothing to back it up. If we were hearing the truth about morality at Mass, it was flying by us. A lot of my time in Mass was spent daydreaming: thinking about what I was going to do for the week, what I was going to do for the day. It was just a time to go and think of other things!

GREG: We knew enough to try to conceal our living together from Julie's parents. They came to visit — it was a surprise visit — for Thanksgiving. We tried to make it look as if we were not living together. Later they found out. One of the things that really hurt her dad was the fact that we had all gone to Mass together and Julie and I received Communion. In my ignorance, I wasn't able to understand why that was wrong. I just thought, "This is what you do when you go to church."

Julie and I were married in 1987 by a Catholic priest. They didn't tell us anything in Pre-Cana that challenged the way we were living. I had no idea that premarital sex and contraception were against the teaching of the Church. I had never really heard anything about Church teaching; I had never even heard the term "Church teaching"! All the Church meant to me was that I went to a ceremony every Sunday. We never prayed. We went to Mass sometimes, and that was just an external thing. We went to Confession twice a year in order to remain Catholic: we knew that we had to do that, but didn't know why. I didn't have a clear understanding at that point of the difference between mortal and venial sin.

At least we realized that we were entering into a commitment to spend the rest of our lives together. We never really thought about divorce. In fact, if there was anything that I *did* know about my Faith, it was that Catholics were not supposed to divorce. But we were using contraception, and sex to us was something for personal pleasure. The message we got from society was that this was okay.

When our first child, Christopher, was born, we knew he had to be baptized. It didn't mean anything to us, but we knew that was what we were supposed to do.

I was in the Army then. About a year after we were married, I was transferred to Denver, where Julie was from. We began to spend a lot of time with her parents. That's when I got a chance to see how devout Catholics lived. I began to see in it something that I wanted. Her parents were happy. They were always caring for other people. Her dad talked about the Faith and about how we should be living our lives. Other people looked up to them. They had something that made me want to be like them.

Nothing much changed in our behavior at that time, but we knew that there was something better — and that Julie's parents had it. We had no idea what we needed to do to be that way.

How our marriage went sour

JULIE: We had stopped contracepting — not because we thought there was anything wrong with it, but because we wanted to have children. Our daughter Lauren was born on December 13, 1989. That's when our life began to change for the worse. The doctor encouraged us to choose sterilization, and Greg got a vasectomy.

GREG: That's when a lot of the problems began — an inability to communicate. We started to argue all the time.

Of course, when we would read the pop-psychology books, they would tell us that we were just entering the disillusionment stage of our relationship and that we were waking up and seeing each other for who we really were. Sex became less frequent: Julie lost interest. Looking back now, we know that it was because she felt used, although she was not communicating that at that time.

JULIE: Everyone else — all my friends, everyone I'd ever known — was contracepting; it was no big deal. But I know that subconsciously, our marital embrace was registering as a negative thing — as rejection!

That was also the way I felt before we were married. We were having sex, and I just thought that those negative feelings must be how people ordinarily feel after they have sex. I felt the same weird, negative feeling after Greg got his vasectomy. Cohabitation and premarital sex brought a negative element into our marriage. It never went away, and after Greg got his vasectomy, it became stronger: I had a sense of being used.

Then Greg got a job in Austin, and we moved away from my parents in Denver.

GREG: Then money entered our life. We thought that money could fix any problems in our relationship. We bought our first home, a car, and even a boat. We felt that these things would help our marriage. We were listening to society: got to have the house, the car, take the trips, get all the toys. That became our focus. That became our god. We pursued these things. I was always looking for ways to make more money.

JULIE: My friends convinced me that staying at home with the kids was unfulfilling. I got a job in sales, making more money than I had ever made in my life. I was the number-one sales person!

But that also made our relationship more negative. I got my affirmation at work. There I felt important. I got the paycheck. I got the bonus money. I was told I was wonderful.

GREG: Julie would get up at five o'clock in the morning, work out, then come and get the kids, put them in daycare, and go to work. After work, she would work out again and get home at 8:30 or nine o'clock every evening. She was working in sales for a health club around very vain people all the time. Money and looks were the things that were important.

One day I woke up. Even though we were attaining all these things, I was still not happy. I was lonely. Julie was never home. It wasn't worth the money.

Julie wouldn't hear of changing our lifestyle. I became depressed. I wasn't motivated to get up and go to work. Julie saw that as my being lazy. She thought I was giving her the responsibility to be the breadwinner. She started to work even longer hours.

Our relationship hits bottom

JULIE: We were not there for each other. We started looking to other people. I started to have lunch with other guys. Greg would spend time with other girls. It was no big deal. We were just friends! Everybody has friends, right? Opposite sex? That's no big deal. Everybody said that!

But we see now that it was infidelity: emotional infidelity. Adultery. Some people say, "Oh, it's no big deal. This guy has been in my life for years. He's a good friend, and it's just a platonic relationship." That always causes problems. For both of us, it soon became sexual infidelity.

GREG: We became so entrenched in sin that we even began to deny the fact that we were sinning in the first place.

JULIE: Even though I was living a sinful life, I agreed to teach religious education! The priest in our new parish had been coming to us, asking us to participate. So I volunteered to teach religious education to Lauren's third-grade class.

But then I accepted a job in San Antonio, which is an hour away from Austin. The money was good, but I also took the job so that Greg and I wouldn't have to deal with each other. It was an escape. I came home on Wednesday nights and weekends, and Greg stayed home and worked at his own job.

GREG: When Julie accepted the job in San Antonio, I replaced her as the religious-education teacher. There, despite my sins, I began to feel God's grace as I learned about the Faith. Everything from that third-grade book had an effect on me. I asked myself the questions I asked my class: *Where is God in your life? How important is God to you? How do you experience God? How do you pray?* All the things that I was supposed to be teaching started lingering in my mind: I thought to myself, "Well, I'm asking these kids to be holy, and I'm not doing it!" I was beginning to feel the need for something more in our life than just money. I was beginning to feel the need for God.

JULIE: But at the same time, our marriage was going from bad to worse. Greg stopped me one day and said, "This is ridiculous."

GREG: Julie came home one Wednesday night, and I told her, "This is enough. We need to stop playing this game. You're unhappy, and I'm unhappy. We need to get a divorce."

JULIE: I agreed. We even called the kids into the room and told them. They were seven and nine. The news devastated them. I remember them both balled up in a corner, crying.

We needed help. We went to our priest for the first time and talked to him about our situation. We didn't want to get divorced without being able to say that we'd done everything we could to avoid getting one.

GREG: We always knew Catholics shouldn't get divorced.

JULIE: So we told our priest that we didn't want to continue the marriage. He referred us to a Christian counselor, who said that maybe we weren't meant to be together. He asked us to schedule a second appointment, but we walked out of there knowing we wouldn't be back: we'd heard what we thought we wanted to hear. Still, deep down inside, we didn't want to part.

We discover life in an unexpected place

GREG: So we did nothing. We thought we shouldn't be together, but we weren't doing anything to separate. We just co-existed and avoided each other.

This went on for about six months. In the summer of 1999, a visiting priest came to our parish. We began to develop a special friendship with him. We later found out that he was the judicial vicar for the diocese, and if we knew anything about our Faith, we knew that this was the guy who ruled on annulments. So we thought, "What better person to ask than the judicial vicar to see what we needed to do to get out of this relationship?"

JULIE: I called to schedule an appointment, and we spent forty-five minutes explaining to him why we couldn't continue our marriage. When we had finished, he said, "I understand that you're miserable and that you think you can't do this anymore. But before you make any further decisions on getting a divorce, I want to ask you a couple of questions:

What is God's plan for marriage? What does the Church teach about marriage? What do the writings of St. Paul say about marriage?"

I said, "What are you talking about? I have no idea! All we know is that we're miserable. We can't stay in this marriage. Can't you show us how to get out of it?"

The priest said, "Before you go any further, I would like you to go home and do some studying." Thank God, Greg did what he said.

GREG: I went back and got the Bible out. I went to Ephesians. Of course, I found the scripture where Paul says, "Wives, be submissive to your husbands." I remember thinking to myself, "Here's the problem! She's not doing anything I tell her to do! She always wants to work, always wants to be away, always wants to do her own thing."

But then I saw, "Husbands, love your wives as Christ loved the Church." So then I started to reflect: Am I doing what I need to do? What did Christ do for the Church? Christ died for the Church! Am I dying to myself for some of the things that Julie wants to do? No.

We had a *Catechism* at home, although we'd never bothered to read it. I looked up what the Church had to say about marriage. A whole new world opened up for me. The Church understood our situation! I read that "it can seem difficult, even impossible, to bind oneself for life to another human being." But God's "definitive and irrevocable love" will "support and sustain" us as we sacrifice ourselves for each other.[18] Never before had I thought about God's love as giving me the power

---

[18] *Catechism of the Catholic Church* (CCC), par. 1648.

to get through tough times — or about my selfishness as a source of trouble in our marriage.

For two days, I continued to read. I got on the Internet and started downloading Church documents. I got *Familiaris Consortio* to see what the Holy Father said about marriage and the family. He talked about "the pressures coming above all from the mass media," causing the "obscuring of certain fundamental values."[19] I was beginning to realize what those values were, and how they had been totally obscured in our lives. We had fallen hook, line, and sinker for society's view of marriage, which is fundamentally selfish: get out of the marriage if you aren't getting pleasure out of it anymore. Never before had I realized that some things were more important than personal gratification — and that a greater happiness could come from self-sacrifice. Never before had I realized that the path to a good marriage lay in *not* insisting on getting my own way.

I felt like St. Paul being knocked off his horse.

JULIE: Greg called me into the room. He said, "Look at what our Church teaches. Look at God's plan for life! No wonder our marriage is messed up. We're not living it at all the way God intended. No wonder we're miserable!" He started teaching me.

GREG: I turned to Julie and said, "We have to pray."

She said, "What do you mean?"

I said, "We have to pray about our situation."

I grabbed her hand, and we got on our knees. Our prayer was this: "God, we have tried living life based on the things that we felt were important. We tried living our marriage the way that society says is right. And as You know, it isn't

[19] *Familiaris Consortio*, par. 7.

working! We invite You into our lives to show us how You want us to live this thing called marriage. If You will deliver us from this evil, we will commit the rest of our lives to working in this kind of ministry."

JULIE: After that prayer, we had to go to Confession. Not just to "follow the rules" and remain Catholic; we knew we had to seek healing and forgiveness with God if we were ever going to have healing and forgiveness in our marriage. We went to our parish church and received the Sacrament of Reconciliation. It was unbelievable! When the priest said, "I absolve you," I felt so light, so free.

GREG: It was as if all the weight of our selfishness and infidelity had been lifted off forever. We were able to start again, to rebuild our relationship with God — and with each other.

After that, God went to work! It was as if our souls were on fire. We kept wanting more, so we'd go back to the books. Even though we had heard of Jesus' Presence in the Eucharist, we never really understood it. Now we were learning about how it would give us the strength to make our marriage work. We were learning about that and every other aspect of our Faith.

We dedicate ourselves to Christ and His Church

JULIE: And we quit our jobs.

GREG: It was about a week later. We saw that materialism and selfishness were our gods. To improve our relationship, everything had to go: jobs, money, friends, whatever — it had to go.

At this point, we were both working for an advertising company. We went in and turned in our resignation letters, and our boss asked, "What are you guys going to do?"

We told him, "Well, we don't know right now."

He said, "You're crazy. You're leaving all this money and going out to nowhere?"

I said, "Well, we used to be crazy. I like to think that now we're gaining a little bit of sanity."

We walked out holding hands and looked up at the sky. We said to God, "Okay, we're Yours. What do You want to do with us?"

While we waited and prayed for a clear answer to that question, we worked selling a weight-loss program out of a trailer. Every day I'd go to the trailer with the Bible, the *Catechism*, and various documents I had downloaded from the Internet. Between customers, I would read — eight to ten hours a day for three months.

Then one night I felt a strong sense that now God wanted me to do something with this knowledge. After our parish priest preached a strong sermon about answering God's call, Julie and I agreed that it was time. We created The Alexander House of Austin, a nonprofit organization to teach people the things that we were learning. We've dedicated ourselves to education for the enrichment of marriage and family life. We also ended up working with, and becoming for a time the directors of, the Family Life Office of the Diocese of Austin.

At that time, I was reading *Humanae Vitae*, Pope Paul VI's encyclical letter on contraception. Until I read it, I had never thought of sterilization and contraception as being the same thing. So I went to Julie and said, "We have another problem." So of course I went to Confession. The priest told me that because at the time I got the vasectomy I was ignorant of the Church's teaching, I wasn't required to have that procedure reversed.

But I thought that there was no way that I could work in the Family Life Office or continue our ministry while remaining in the state I was in. So with Julie, I prayed, "God, I know what the Church teaches. I think I'm in a state of grace. However, I'm still not sure what I should do about this vasectomy. If You're asking me to reverse it, I need You to show me a sign."

We got the sign when we got back to Austin from a marriage conference in Denver. We went to see a doctor who did reversals, and he was so excited by our ministry that he offered to charge us only five hundred dollars for the operation! Reversals can cost five to ten thousand dollars or more.

Almost nine months to the day after I had the procedure was Father's Day. Julie gave me a card. Inside was a positive pregnancy test! Nine months later, our daughter Katharine was born. Now we understand totally why a child is a gift from God.

JULIE: We do workshops and seminars on God's plan for marriage and God's plan for sex. We also do marriage coaching. We have met with more than two hundred couples in the last two years, and we have taught every single one the importance of the Sacrament of Reconciliation and of the Presence of Jesus in the Eucharist.

God's grace has touched a few of them in particular. About twelve couples have come to us and told us that because of our story and what we've told them about the Church's teaching on contraception, they are going off the Pill or are looking into getting a reversal.

What we tell people about controversial Church teachings

GREG: They just don't know any better. That's why we continue our ministry. People come to us all the time and ask questions such as "What's wrong with living together before marriage? Isn't it more responsible to make sure you're compatible before entering into a lifelong relationship?"

We rely on the teachings of the Holy Father to answer them. In *Familiaris Consortio*, he says that sexuality "is by no means something purely biological, but concerns the innermost being of the human person as such. It is realized in a truly human way only if it is an integral part of the love by which a man and a woman commit themselves totally to one another until death. The total physical self-giving would be a lie if it were not the sign and fruit of a total personal self-giving: if the person were to withhold something or reserve the possibility of deciding otherwise in the future, by this very fact he or she would not be giving totally."[20]

That means that premarital sex and living together before marriage actually harm a marriage by starting it off with a lie. Contraception and sterilization continue and amplify that lie. Sooner or later, the strain of all this dishonesty will start to show in the relationship. All intimacy is threatened, and the couple may stop trusting each other altogether — their oneness is broken. That's what happened to us.

But even though they bring the same kinds of problems into a relationship, premarital sex and contraception are usually not connected in people's minds. Sometimes in our workshops, we get married couples who are living as good Catholics as far as they know: they didn't engage in premarital sex, but they're contracepting. We address the problems with contraception in a workshop called "Marriage Takes Three." We start out by talking about God's plan for marriage versus the

---

[20] *Familiaris Consortio*, no. 11.

expectations of society. We explain to them why Natural Family Planning (NFP) is not the same as contraception because it doesn't impede the total self-giving of the couple. If you limit intercourse to the infertile periods of a woman's cycle, you're not acting against God's design for men and women, and for marriage. God has created a woman's natural cycle of fertility and infertility; with NFP, you're respecting His design, instead of overriding it. When you're contracepting, you're using the sexual act for the pleasure involved, but you're withholding from one another an important aspect of yourself. Through your bodies, you're communicating that your love is not total and unconditional. It's for better but not for worse.

We've all heard about how important it is to communicate. And as John Paul II says, the marital embrace is the ultimate means of communicating life and love to your spouse. If you're contracepting, you're cutting that off. How can you expect the rest of your marriage relationship to work?

We discovered the truth of that long before we learned it intellectually. On reflection, we started to realize that a lot of our problems began after the vasectomy. When we had decided to cut God out of that part of our lives, we also cut ourselves off from His grace. In the Sacrament of Matrimony, God has given us all the grace we need to be successful in our marriages — provided that we live out our marriage the way He intended.

JULIE: So many Catholics want to get rid of the crucifix. They want to see the risen Christ in their churches. But if you look at the crucifix, it's the perfect example of love. If we understand that, it will help our relationships and our marriages. Because that is love: to die to ourselves, to give life to somebody else.

GREG: We always quote *Gaudium et Spes* from Vatican II: "Man can only fully realize himself when he's able to make a sincere gift of self." It's all about self-giving. When we give to our spouse, only then can we begin to understand who we are. That is imitating Christ. He was always devoted to giving, not to looking to see what He could get out of things. In this light, we can see how it makes sense to say that a husband and wife are called to be an icon of Christ and the Church.

JULIE: So often today, people want the Church to conform to their lives, instead of making an effort to conform their lives to the Church, and to live the way that the Church has intended. But we have to go back and understand why we are here in the first place. We're made for truth, and we're made for love. Truth is Jesus Christ, not what we think truth is. It is found only in Him. And God is love. We try drugs, sex, material things — but truth and love can never be found in those things. As St. Augustine said, "Our hearts cannot rest until they rest in Thee."[21]

We make less money than we've ever made in our lives. Yet we're richer now than we've ever been.

GREG: People ask us, "Why do you do what you do?" I tell them, "Whenever Christ heals someone, He asks them to go out and tell people what He has done for them." That's what we've dedicated our lives to doing!

[21] St. Augustine, *Confessions*, Bk. 1, ch. 1.

I Was Almost Left Behind

When I was young, I was taught that true Christians would one day be "raptured" into Heaven. Then I found that the Rapture and many Protestant teachings have no basis in the Bible.

Carl E. Olson

I stood in the kitchen doorway, a four-year-old taking a break from playing with my toys.

"Mom," I said, "are you and Dad going to Heaven when you die?"

My mother turned to look at me, her hands covered in flour.

"Yes, we are. Why do you ask?"

"Am I going to Heaven when I die?"

She knelt down and looked at me intently.

"That depends, Carl."

"On what?" I felt anxious. I knew what happened to people who didn't go to Heaven.

"On whether you've accepted Jesus into your heart as your personal Savior. Have you done that?" She knew that I hadn't.

"No."

"Do you want to?"

I nodded.

She led me into my bedroom, and we knelt at my bed. We had never knelt like that before, but I knew that I was about to do something very important.

"Carl, you need to pray to Jesus and ask Him into your heart. Tell Him that you are sorry for your sins and you want to be saved."

I was quiet. I didn't know what to say.

"You can repeat after me, okay?" She smiled at me, and I nodded, suddenly nervous. She closed her eyes, and I did the same.

"Dear Jesus . . ." she began. I repeated after her.

"Please forgive me for my sins. Thank You for dying for my sins so that I can go to Heaven. Please come into my heart. I want You to be my personal Savior. Amen."

At that moment, I knew I was saved. And I knew that someday I would be with my parents in Heaven. We got up, I went back outside to play, and my mother finished making bread.

Born again in rural Montana

Both of my parents were raised in rural South Dakota and had difficult upbringings. My mother was the fifth child in a farming family of fourteen kids — eleven of whom were girls. The only respite from the constant chores and housework was Sunday morning at the local Lutheran church. Years later, my mother told me, with obvious distaste, of the "man-made ritual and hypocrisy" she witnessed there. In fact, she insisted that the Lutheran and Catholic Churches were cut from the same apostate, non-biblical cloth, filled with worthless ritual, empty words, and pathetic gestures.

Raised in the beautiful Black Hills of South Dakota, my father and his four siblings barely scraped by on the money earned by their father, a construction worker who was rarely home. When my father was just fourteen, he was informed by a neighbor that his father had just died of leukemia. He and his siblings were never told that their father was ill or why their mother was gone at the time. This stoic Scandinavian upbringing didn't encourage communication, but it did shape hard-working boys who had few illusions about how tough life could be. After high school, my father worked as a sawyer and a welder, eventually ending up in central South Dakota, where he met my mother.

Married and looking for employment, my parents eventually settled in western Montana. Not long before I was born, my parents were "born again," and they began attending a small Church of God service — a mildly Pentecostal Fundamentalist affair with traditional hymns and lengthy sermons. Shortly after my birth, they switched to an equally small Christian and Missionary Alliance gathering that met in the upstairs loft of the Odd Fellows Hall on Main Street.

It was there, in a plain room with a small stage at front, that my first memories of "church" were formed. Every Sunday morning, a group of about forty people would gather for Sunday school, followed by a simple service of hymns, some extemporaneous prayers, and a thirty-minute sermon. At just three or four years old, we were expected to memorize Scripture verses every week and recite them in front of the congregation.

Small differences make for a multitude of divisions

At the age of five, I experienced my first church split — the first of several I would witness over the next twenty years. The pastor of our small group was generally well liked; however, he believed that Christians could lose their salvation, which some members of our group did not accept. (Anyone familiar with Fundamentalism and Evangelical Protestantism knows how controversial this topic is.) So a handful of families, ours among them, split off and formed a small home church. The goal was to return to the New Testament roots and emulate, as best as possible, the actions and teachings of the first Christians, based upon Acts 2:42: "And they devoted themselves to the Apostles' teaching and fellowship, to the breaking of bread and the prayers." Based on this passage, our home services consisted of Scripture reading, an informal sermon, a simple communion service with grape juice and bread, and a closing prayer.

There were only a little over a thousand residents in my hometown, but there were about a dozen Christian or pseudo-Christian groups: Christian and Missionary Alliance, Church of God, Assembly of God, Methodist, Lutheran, Baptist, Catholic, Mormons, Jehovah's Witnesses, and a few other small home groups similar to ours. We viewed the other groups with suspicion and even disdain. Although friendly to the Baptists and the more Fundamentalist groups, we had no doubt that the Lutherans and Catholics weren't really Christian. Our attitude toward Pentecostals like those who attended the Assembly of God was condescending. Like every good Bible Christian, we knew that the gifts of the Holy Spirit had ceased in the first century, and those who indulged in such immature and emotional actions were to be pitied for failing to recognize this.

We were separatist in the truest sense of the word. We set ourselves up as final arbiters of Christian orthodoxy, convinced that a plain and commonsensical reading of the Bible was the only way to be truly Christian, free from the entanglements of tradition, human wisdom, and secularism.

Fervent Fundamentalism: a view from inside

The term *fundamentalism* has, unfortunately, been abused and distorted by those unfamiliar with its origins. Often used in a negative sense today, it was first used — and still is by those who gladly accept the label — to describe conservative Protestants who hold to the "fundamentals" of the Christian faith, in opposition to the rising tide of modern biblical criticism and the liberal notions about God, Jesus Christ, and sin making their way into mainstream Protestant churches. Fundamentalists believe in the divinity of Jesus Christ, the reality of sin, the need for salvation, the inspiration of sacred Scripture, the Virgin Birth, and the imminent return of Jesus Christ in glory. As Fundamentalists, we would have little to do with anything that we deemed worldly or unbiblical.

The difficulty was that members of our group had differing views about what was worldly and what was not. Some families refused to own, or even watch, a television, while others had no such qualms. Similar tensions arose about music, books, movies, and other forms of entertainment. Our family didn't own a television until I was in high school (for which I'm still grateful), but my parents allowed me to watch certain approved shows — some cartoons and sports — at the homes of friends. Now that I am a parent, I can appreciate my parents' concern and caution. But there was a palpable sense of fear, even paranoia, about worldly activities and entertainment.

For example, when I was six or seven, some teenagers in another family wanted to read *The Chronicles of Narnia*. They insisted that the books were harmless fantasy, but their concerned parents brought the issue before the entire group and asked for the opinions of the elders. Someone offered that the books were written by a Christian, that they were in fact an allegory about Christ and salvation. I'll never forget the response of one of the elders, who vehemently declared, "If people want to read about Jesus Christ, they can read the Bible. We don't need allegories!"

The group also forbade playing cards, drinking alcohol of any sort, and dancing. One of my more embarrassing memories from childhood was bringing a note from my parents to my junior-high gym class, informing my teacher that I was not allowed to participate in square dancing. I recall watching friends playing cribbage and wanting to learn how to play, but I knew it was off limits. In their fervor and desire to be good Christians, my parents often overreacted and made decisions that were extreme. But looking back, I see that they weren't afraid of standing out, of being different, or of appearing foolish for their beliefs, and I respect that. This courage was a tremendous influence on how I approached my faith, and it played a vital role years later when I questioned the premises and presuppositions of my Protestant heritage.

Catholics and the end of the world

"Why aren't Catholics and Lutherans saved?" I once asked my mother. I knew they weren't saved, but I wasn't sure why.

"There are many reasons," she replied. "One is that they don't believe in the book of Revelation. They deny it is the Word of God."

"What do you mean?"

"They say it isn't true. They believe it is only symbolic and has nothing to do with the end times."

"But don't they have the same Bible as we do?" As a sixth-grader, I was increasingly interested in what other people believed and in their reasons for rejecting Christianity.

"Maybe," she shrugged, "but they don't believe in it."

In junior high, I developed into a tall, lanky basketball player. I also developed a fascination with the book of Revelation, the Rapture, and the end of the world. I read Hal Lindsey's best-selling books, *The Late Great Planet Earth* and *There's a New World Coming*. I listened to tapes by Jack van Impe, a Fundamentalist teacher known as "The Walking Bible." Both men wrote and spoke in breathless, excited tones about the return of Jesus, who was going to "snatch out" the Christians from the world prior to a seven-year period of tribulation. This "Rapture" event was a major focus for our small group — we now called ourselves a "Bible Chapel" — and I heard numerous talks and sermons about it and about the rapidly approaching end of the world, the rise of the Antichrist, and the great apostasy already conquering most of so-called Christianity.

Catholics, of course, were highest on our list of false Christians. I enjoyed reading the lurid, colorful Jack Chick comic books, filled with stories about the horrors of the Catholic Church, the torture of nuns and innocent people, and the Church's proclamation of a false gospel of works, rituals, and bizarre practices.

The two families I was closest to in junior high and high school were nominally Catholic. They were wonderful people, but through many conversations with them about Jesus and the Bible, it became clear to me that they knew nothing about either, confirming the emptiness of Catholicism. The Catholics I went to school with didn't exhibit any of the qualities I expected of Christians; in fact, they partied, fornicated, and swore just as freely as everyone else. Our view of the Catholic Church seemed validated by these Catholics.

But none of this was surprising, because Scripture and Bible-prophecy experts argued that the Catholic Church was most likely the Whore of Babylon described in the book of Revelation. Especially disturbing to us was the claim that Catholics taught that we had to earn salvation, rather than accepting it as a free gift of God's grace. It never occurred to me at the time that Jack Chick, Bart Brewer, and the other anti-Catholic authors I was reading might be distorting what the Catholic Church actually taught. I couldn't have fathomed that there are Catholics who read their Bibles, that the Catholic Church doesn't teach "works righteousness," and that the Catholic Church was founded by Jesus Christ.

In art I find echoes of the divine

From the age of three, I had been a voracious reader. My mother read me books meant for children older than I, so I skipped a few years of reading material. In fifth grade, I mixed Shakespeare's *Julius Caesar*, the *Hardy Boys* series, John Milton's *Paradise Lost*, and the *Encyclopedia Brown* books with Charles Dickens' *Oliver Twist* and *David Copperfield*, and a Bible correspondence study course from Fundamentalist publisher David C. Cook! In addition, I discovered I had a talent for drawing, which led me to discover Rembrandt, Michelangelo, Andrew Wyeth, Norman Rockwell, and other artists. I was slowly being exposed to other world views and other perceptions about the world, reality, and the nature of man.

Like many teenagers, I went through some tempestuous times during high school. My artwork caused tension with my parents. From the time I had started drawing, they had encouraged me to paint scenery and wildlife, subjects that were popular and sold well. But I was convinced I would need to take up more serious subject matters if I was going to be a true artist. While a freshman in high school, I read and reread *My Name Is Asher Lev*, by the Jewish novelist Chaim Potok. It is the story of a young Orthodox Jewish painter and his struggle to reconcile his Jewish faith with his art, a struggle that led him to break from his parents and from Judaism.

I wasn't considering walking away from Christianity, but I was frustrated by the limited view of the arts within Christianity as I knew it. I thought that good art needed no justification: if it was good, it deserved to exist. Fundamentalism, however, had a utilitarian approach: art was supposed to be "functional," as though beauty needed a reason to exist other than its own goodness. I see now that I was developing a sense of an incarnational, sacramental view of reality, nurtured by the poetry of T. S. Eliot, the Anglo-Catholic man of letters whose poems are filled with a powerful, mystical vision of the Incarnation.

On my own, I learn to defend my faith

A few weeks after graduating from high school, I moved to Phoenix and enrolled in an intensive one-year course in graphic design. I wanted to learn about commercial art, find a decent job, and spend my spare time painting. After just a few days in the Valley of the Sun, I realized that things out in the world weren't going to be so easy. I was homesick and depressed. Although I did well in my studies, I became despondent and was close to packing up and leaving. One day I came home from school, went into the bathroom, lay on the floor, and wept for what seemed to be an eternity. At that moment, I started praying as I never had before in my life.

My year in Phoenix forced me to turn to God and to trust in Him completely. I began to memorize large sections of

Scripture and spent time in prayer every day, a practice my parents had encouraged but I had never been successful at before. Each morning I would read several of the Psalms. Little did I know that I was practicing what the Catholic Church had been doing for two thousand years: following the Jewish practice of praying the Psalms on a daily basis.

While my spiritual life flourished, the intellectual basis for my belief in God and Christianity was being called into question. I was surrounded by students and teachers who openly mocked and attacked Christianity. One teacher in particular had an intense dislike for "organized religion" — namely, Christianity. He claimed that early Christians had destroyed most of the real sayings and teachings of Christ — the "Gnostic scriptures" — and that the Church was simply a group of old men getting wealthy off simpleminded folk. I tried to put up a fight, but quickly realized that I knew almost nothing about the early Christians, the Gnostics, or how the Bible was put together.

On most afternoons, I would spend time in the pool at my apartment complex. There I met Mike, a forty-something New Age "guru" who was convinced that he was called to save the world. We spent hours talking about Christianity, often arguing about the existence of God and whether Jesus was God. (Mike's opinion: Jesus was God, but so are we all.) I was never satisfied with my replies and knew there had to be better responses available. These conversations, combined with my confrontations with classmates and teachers, showed me how little I actually knew about Christian theology and other, competing world views.

After my year in Phoenix, I returned home, uncertain of my next step. After years of leadership from volunteer elders, my home church had just hired a full-time pastor, Joel. He and I quickly became good friends. We had the same taste in music, and he was as eager to teach me about Christian apologetics as I was to learn. He introduced me to C. S. Lewis, Francis Schaeffer, and some lesser-known Protestant apologists and writers. Joel encouraged me to consider attending Bible college for a year, but I resisted. I thought it would slow my artistic progress, and I pictured Bible college as a dreary, humorless place full of overly pious people. But I knew that I needed spiritual guidance and formation; I also liked the fact that the Bible college that Joel recommended had a basketball team. So, with mixed motives and having never seen Briercrest Bible College (BBC), I headed off to Saskatchewan, Canada. It would be a turning point in my life. As I've since said to some of my former classmates: "If I hadn't gone to BBC, I might not be a Catholic today."

Catholic authors and the Covenant at Bible college

Briercrest was founded in the 1930s as a Fundamentalist Bible college. By the time I attended it, in the late 1980s, it was a lively mixture of Fundamentalism and Evangelicalism, with even a couple of teachers who selectively embraced elements of Catholic and Anglo-Catholic theology. Like most small Bible colleges in North America, BBC was a hotbed of premillennial dispensationalist theology: teaching the inevitable failure of the Church, the necessity of the saving Rapture event for "true believers," and the eventual thousand-year earthly reign of Jesus Christ. Many of the teachers simply assumed this to be the case — it was *the* "biblical" scenario based on a selective group of verses drawn from Revelation, Matthew,

Daniel, and 1 Thessalonians. But I soon discovered that my favorite teacher, Mr. Winter, had other ideas.

Mr. Winter taught courses on the Old Testament, including the Pentateuch, the historical books, and the prophets. Knowledgeable in ancient near-Middle Eastern history, he developed his theology of Old Testament thought from his understanding of the culture and practices common to that time and place. In other words, he did not bring a theology to the texts, but tried to understand the texts in the context of history. The result was an unusual — for a Fundamentalist Bible college — emphasis on the centrality of covenant. He demonstrated that without at least a cursory knowledge of the covenants with Abraham, Moses, and David, a Christian couldn't really appreciate the new covenant founded by Jesus Christ. A few years later, I would listen to a former Protestant, Scott Hahn, explain how the teachings and practice of the Catholic Church bring out the riches and glory of the covenant, and how the new covenant is fulfilled by Christ in His Church.

Although he was quiet about it, Mr. Winter did not adhere to the common belief in the Rapture and the dispensationalist system taught by other teachers. He didn't have a fully formed idea of end-times events, but did have serious reservations about the belief in the Rapture and the earthly millennium. For the first time in my life, I heard a devout Christian call into doubt a belief that I had always considered as biblical as the Incarnation, sin, and the grace of God. It was a small taste of things to come.

In my humanities courses, I was reading T. S. Eliot, Flannery O'Connor, Graham Greene, and the Jesuit poet Gerard Manley Hopkins. These writers had a profound grasp of the realities of sin, grace, and free will. My literature professor, who leaned toward the Anglican Church, encouraged us to attend an Anglican or Catholic Mass in order to experience the beauty of the Liturgy. Those were the first positive remarks I had ever heard about the practice of the Catholic Church. One of my favorite classes was apologetics; it addressed agnosticism and atheism and whetted my appetite for future studies of philosophy. For the first time, I heard about St. Thomas Aquinas and his five proofs for the existence of God. We also read select portions of St. Augustine's *Confessions*; it was never mentioned, however, that St. Augustine was a Catholic bishop who believed in all of the Catholic doctrines we found abhorrent: the Real Presence of Christ in the Eucharist, the teaching authority of the Church, and the sacraments.

I develop doubts and an incarnational view of reality

In the autumn of 1991, after two years at BBC, I moved to Oregon to look for work in graphic design. Shortly after arriving in Portland, I met Heather, who was a student at Multnomah Bible College. After we started dating, we attended a couple of Evangelical churches and finally settled into one we thought was biblically sound. During this time, I formed a friendship with Joel's father, Richard, a retired Fundamentalist pastor who lived in the Portland area. He and I spent time discussing Scripture and ideas about church authority and doctrine. He emphatically believed that "true" churches had no structure or organization, but were meant to be small home meetings led by the Holy Spirit and based on the final authority of Scripture — the same belief with which I had been raised.

Although I enjoyed our conversations, I was starting to question both the logic and attitude behind his opinions — opinions that were foundational for Fundamentalists and many Evangelicals. One day, for example, while visiting with my cousin's wife, I asked her why she attended an Episcopalian church.

"Well, I really enjoy the service there," she said.

"Is that the best reason to attend a church?" I asked.

She seemed puzzled and asked, "Why do you attend the church you do?"

"Because it teaches the Bible," I replied.

"How do you know it teaches the Bible correctly?" she innocently responded.

"Because there are certain hermeneutical and exegetical methods you can use to interpret the Bible correctly," I said, thinking this point should be as obvious as night and day.

Her response took me by surprise. "But how do you know *those* methods are correct?"

I tried to explain to her how the true meaning of the Bible is clear to true Christians. But the logical implications stuck with me. How could I be certain that what my church taught was more correct than what any other church taught? How could true Christians differ so widely over the interpretations of so many passages of Scripture?

There were Scripture passages that had puzzled me while I was attending BBC, but they had never been explained to my satisfaction. One was John 3:5 and the meaning of being born of "the water and the Spirit." But foremost in my mind was the sixth chapter of John. I read it repeatedly, the words haunting me: "Truly, truly, I say to you, unless you eat the Flesh of the Son of Man and drink His Blood, you have no life in you."[22] I was well aware of the metaphorical interpretation common among most Protestants, but I thought it was rather weak, especially in light of a passage such as 1 Corinthians 11:23-32. I had been fortunate to grow up in a group that observed weekly communion (albeit a short and informal variety), and I saw a disparity between the emphasis of Scripture and the reality of how I experienced communion.

A few months after moving to Portland, I developed a strong interest in politics, especially the history of political thought in Western culture. This was the beginning of a journey into Catholic social thought and teaching. I began reading the works of Russell Kirk, whose emphasis on what he called the "permanent things" and his understanding of the place of Christianity in the history of political thought fascinated me. Through Kirk I was exposed further to the logic of St. Thomas Aquinas, the scholarship of John Henry Newman, and the wit of G. K. Chesterton. I began to wonder why it was the Catholics and Anglo-Catholics who had so much to say about the relationship of the Christian Faith to politics and society.

Chesterton's *Orthodoxy* was even more thought-provoking. This dazzling apologetic for Christianity against the errors of modern philosophies showed me how central "paradox" is to the Christian Faith. True Christianity is a radical balance of "both/and" instead of just "either/or." Jesus Christ is both God *and* man; God is both one *and* three; the Church is both holy *and* made up of sinners. Of course, Protestants agree with at least the first two propositions. But many, especially Fundamentalists, insist on adhering to the Bible only — not

[22] John 6:53.

Scripture *and* Tradition. Likewise, they believe they are saved by faith alone, not by faith *and* works performed by God's grace. These distinctions helped me better to understand core Catholic teachings and further appreciate the mystery of the Incarnation.

Then I read *The Everlasting Man*, Chesterton's study of the Incarnation and its effect on human history, which showed me how large, how breathtaking, how incarnational the Catholic view of reality is, compared with the often pitiful perspectives I held. I was getting glimpses into the larger world of Catholic thought, a world so large that it was frightening and so intimate that it was comforting. As I considered the reality of the Incarnation, I recognized the logic and beauty of a sacramental faith in which God works through physical matter, not just through spiritual impulse. Although I wasn't ready to give the Catholic Church too much credit, I knew it was certainly not the "Whore of Babylon." If the Catholic Church did indeed propagate false teachings, it also had a handle on some important truths.

During this time, I was becoming frustrated over a steady stream of Fundamentalist and Evangelical books proclaiming the collapse of the American economy, the rise of the Antichrist, and the imminent Rapture. I had been hearing such things since I was a young child, and I knew that similar prophets of doom had sung the same tune decades earlier. I was tired of the pessimism I so often found in Protestantism. Where was the peace and contentment spoken of by Jesus and Paul? Where was the joy of Chesterton? I was no longer able to handle the constant doom-and-gloom scenarios and the lack of balance so prevalent within conservative Protestant circles.

I dare myself to seek answers and find rich profundity

Soon after Heather and I were married in June 1994, I decided it was time to let the Catholic Church speak for herself. What did the Catholic Church actually claim and teach? I went through the religion section of my favorite bookstore. While I was looking at a copy of the recently published *Catechism of the Catholic Church*, another book caught my eye: *Catholicism and Fundamentalism*. I read the back, but wasn't sure whether I should buy it. A young man saw me put it back on the shelf.

"I really recommend that book," he said.

"Which side of this do you fall on?" I asked, referring to the title.

"I used to be a Fundamentalist," he replied, "but I became a Catholic, partly because of that book."

"Really?" I was now curious.

"Yes. In fact, I'm here looking for information on the Trappists. I'm thinking of becoming a monk." We talked for a while longer, and I took his advice and bought the book.

I finished reading *Catholicism and Fundamentalism* the next evening. I was impressed with how well the author, Karl Keating, understood and accurately presented Fundamentalist teachings and showed the inherent flaws of the assumptions behind them. It was as if years of stored-up questions, implications, inferences, and frustrations were flushed out into the open, finally able to be addressed and examined with clarity.

I also read sections of the *Catechism* on salvation, the sacraments, and the role of Mary. I was both surprised and nervous to see how biblical, Christocentric, and Trinitarian the teachings were. I began to see the truth of the *Catechism's* remark that "Mary's role in the Church is inseparable from her union with Christ and flows directly from it."[23] Mary's value cannot be understood apart from her relationship with her Son, and any attempt to do so is bound to fail. The sacramental life began to make sense as I assimilated the Church's teaching that the sacraments are a vital means of participating in Christ's own life: "The fruit of the sacramental life is that the Spirit of adoption makes the faithful partakers in the divine nature by uniting them in a living union with the only Son, the Savior."[24]

Yet a part of me wanted to reject the possibility that the Catholic Church was the true Church, even while another part dared me to continue on in my search for the truth. I still had many questions, especially about salvation and Mary, but I knew I was beginning to find answers. Although Heather was uncertain about this direction, she patiently endured my deepening interest in Catholicism and began to read some of the books I was studying. Nearly every evening, we would talk about how what we were reading compared with what we had been taught while growing up and attending Bible college.

In the months that followed, I began an erratic, but fruitful journey of study and consideration of the Catholic Church. I read the works of Catholic theologians and the documents of the Second Vatican Council. I read conversion stories by those entering the Church, as well as testimonies of anti-Catholics who had left the Church. I read Catholic, Protestant, and secular histories of the early church and the Reformation; I found a couple of volumes of the early Church Fathers and

[23] CCC, par. 964.
[24] CCC, par. 1129.

read those. When I read Ignatius of Antioch,[25] who wrote only eighty years after Christ's death about the reality of Christ's Flesh and Blood in the Eucharist, it was a knife in my heart. Instead of finding an early church that was Protestant, I discovered a Church that believed in the Real Presence of Christ in the Eucharist, baptismal regeneration, liturgical worship, and apostolic succession. Like so many other people who have examined Catholicism, I read John Henry Newman's *The Development of Christian Doctrine*. His famous words burned into my mind: "To be deep in history is to cease to be Protestant."

It could also be said that "to be deep in the Scripture is to cease to be Fundamentalist." This would strike them as ludicrous, but like so many before me, I was seeing Bible verses that I didn't even know existed, and I was discovering, through Catholic doctrine, a rich profundity in the whole of Scripture never obvious to me before. My education in "covenant" was proving useful, especially regarding a matter of central importance to me: the Eucharist. The relationship between the Eucharist as both the sacrificial heart and family core of the New Covenant revealed that the Catholic Church wasn't full of man-made formulas and empty ritual, but was full of life-giving food and drink, the very Body and Blood of my Lord and Savior.

Friends and family intervene, but we go to Mass anyway

Amid the whirlwind of reading and learning, I wrote a letter to Joel, my former pastor. Although I was afraid of what he

---

[25] St. Ignatius of Antioch (d. c. 107), disciple of John the Evangelist, bishop, and martyr.

might say, he was the only person, aside from Heather, whom I thought I could talk to about what I was reading. He expressed serious reservations and concern, but wasn't upset. He was even encouraging, saying, "I believe that you'll only be a better Christian through this study, if you do it carefully."

But when my parents found out I was studying Catholicism, the response was much different. They immediately sent a video by the anti-Catholic "evangelist" James McCarthy, plus some anti-Catholic articles. I watched the video, read the articles, and then wrote a long letter to my parents, going over each point and accusation. All of the criticisms were the result of twisting and misunderstanding Catholic teaching. One of the articles claimed Catholics weren't allowed to read Scripture, while the other claimed that Catholics should be ashamed for not knowing the truth of the Bible, since the Pope encouraged them to read the Bible. "Which is it?" I wrote to my parents. "Both can't be true, yet both are used to damn the Catholic Church. How fair is that?"

Meanwhile, my former classmates and teachers were responding with either complete revulsion or puzzled concern. One friend wrote and told me that her husband had "come out of" the Catholic Church and I should beware of what problems I would find within it. Another told me that I was "over-intellectualizing" my faith and losing sight of the truth. He was convinced that Catholics believed in works-righteousness and taught a false salvation. Almost all of them questioned me about the distinctly Catholic Marian doctrines and the papacy. Of course, explaining these things was never easy, and I rarely felt I succeeded in doing more than upsetting people.

Heather and I still hadn't attended a Catholic Mass, even though we lived across the street from a large Catholic church.

Finally, after weeks of consideration, I called the priest there and set up an appointment. On a cold evening in November 1995, we met with Fr. Tim in his office. I had read stories of priests trying to talk Protestants out of entering the Catholic Church and had no idea of what to expect. I felt better when I saw that he had several books by C. S. Lewis in his bookcase. Heather and I told him our story and said we were interested in getting to know the Church from the "inside."

"My biggest concern is that what I'll actually experience and see will be much different from what I've read and studied," I told him.

"You're welcome to attend Mass anytime," Fr. Tim said, "although you can't take part in the Eucharist." I was glad to hear him say this, since it assured me he had a good understanding of what the Eucharist was, something I knew some Catholics didn't always appreciate as they should.

Leaving his office, Heather and I were relieved, but we also had a growing realization that we were in a no-man's land. We wouldn't go back to the churches we had left, but we both still had concerns and fears about the Catholic Church. We both believed it was important to move slowly (even though some of our friends and family thought we were rushing in). So it wasn't until Easter of 1996 that we attended our first Mass. We liked the sense of quietness and sacredness there, and we started going two or three times a month. That fall we entered the RCIA (Rite of Christian Initiation for Adults) program.

As I studied Catholic theology, I came across areas of the Church's teaching and life that were foreign to me, such as the Church calendar, the feasts, and some of the gestures and actions of the Liturgy. A larger area of concern was that of eschatology. What did the Church believe about the end-times, the

Rapture, and the Antichrist? The *Catechism* addressed these matters, but with great brevity. I was anxious to find a Catholic work that specifically dealt with dispensationalism, the Fundamentalist end-times belief system with the Rapture at its core. I finally came across a chapter in *Born Fundamentalist, Born Again Catholic*, written by ex-Baptist and former Rapture-believer David Currie. Although not in detail, he outlined the basic positions and addressed the larger issues. He also pointed out something that I recently learned, that the concept of a Rapture event separate from the Second Coming was less than two hundred years old. I launched a detailed study of the topic.

The rap on the Rapture

I soon discovered serious historical, theological, and biblical flaws in the dispensationalist system — flaws I once accepted without question. Dispensationalism was invented in the 1830s by anti-Catholic, ex-Anglican priest John Nelson Darby. His central idea was that the church is in deep apostasy. Darby was fond of proclaiming, "The Church is in ruins!" He believed that Jesus had failed in His original mission: the Savior had offered an earthly kingdom to the Jewish people, but they had rejected Him and killed Him. This troubling idea is still taught by dispensationalists today, although many don't do so as openly as Darby did.

Darby taught, and subsequent dispensationalists believe, that the culmination of salvation history will be the removal from earth of the Christian "remnant" (the Rapture), followed by a period of suffering (the "Tribulation"), then a thousand-year reign by Jesus Christ on the earth. During this millennium, the Jews will reign on earth from the earthly Jerusalem while Christians will reign in Heaven in the heavenly Jerusalem. For years I had unknowingly ingested this dualistic view of God's dealings with humanity. As I drew closer to the Catholic Church, I could finally see how odd it really is.

I found that prominent dispensationalists admit that no clear and obvious scriptural support exists for the belief in the Rapture as they teach it. Tim LaHaye, creator of the *Left Behind* books, openly acknowledges the fact that "no one passage of Scripture teaches the two aspects of His Second Coming separated by the Tribulation" and that "no passage teaches a post-Tribulation or mid-Tribulation rapture, either."[26]

The Rapture and the entire dispensationalist system, I learned, are based on Darby's key premise: the existence of two peoples of God. Rapturists begin by assuming that premise, then try to read Scripture in a way that fits their preconceived notions. Despite what supporters say, these notions are based, not on a plain and objective reading of the Bible, but solely on Darby's words.

But what about passages such as 1 Thessalonians 4:16-17, which states, "For the Lord Himself will descend from Heaven with a cry of command, with the archangel's call, and with the sound of the trumpet of God. And the dead in Christ will rise first; then we who are alive, who are left, shall be caught up together with them in the clouds to meet the Lord in the air; and so we shall always be with the Lord." Isn't this passage about the Rapture, as men such as Hal Lindsey, Jack van Impe, and Tim LaHaye consistently teach?

Although St. Paul here clearly refers to believers being "caught up" to "meet the Lord," there is no indication that

---

[26] *Rapture Under Attack*, 75.

this will happen prior to the Tribulation and the Second Coming. Whereas dispensationalists insist that the Rapture will be silent and secret, St. Paul says the very opposite is the case: there is a "cry" uttered by Christ, as well as the call of an archangel and the trumpet of God. A literal interpretation indicates that this event will be both visible and vocal! Some dispensationalists argue that only those who are being raptured will see or hear what is happening. This is convenient, but unconvincing.

What is most striking about this passage is that it provides no evidence at all for the pretribulational Rapture and, in fact, contradicts it. In contrast, Catholics and the vast majority of other Christians believe this passage refers to the Second Coming, when the dead in Christ will rise again. In answering the question "When will the dead rise?" the *Catechism* quotes from the fourth chapter of 1 Thessalonians: "Definitively 'at the last day,' 'at the end of the world.' " Indeed, in 1 Thessalonians 4 the resurrection of the dead is closely associated with the Second Coming.

When I encountered the *Left Behind* books, I was surprised at how prominently they were displayed in non-Christian bookstores. Today, of course, they are the best-selling Christian novels of all time. This is unfortunate, because the books are not only poorly written, but they also spread false beliefs about the Rapture, the end of the world, and the book of Revelation. LaHaye is openly anti-Catholic and often writes in a tone and style that would make Jack Chick proud. In a recent book, he writes, "[T]he Church of Rome denies the finished work of Christ but believes in the continuing sacrifice that produces such things as sacraments and praying for the dead, burning candles, and so forth. All of these were borrowed from mystery Babylon, the mother of all pagan customs and idolatry, none of which is taught in the New Testament."[27] His nonfiction works are filled with similar strident opinions, with few, if any, of them footnoted or explained. Most other proponents of dispensationalism hold similar views. They believe that the Catholic Church is apostate, that the Pope is an antichrist, and that the Vatican is the center of a future worldwide false religion.

In contrast with the hope-filled teachings of the gospel, dispensationalism is reactionary and pessimistic. Popular dispensationalists such as LaHaye and Hal Lindsey have a low view of humanity and are convinced that they, as God's faithful, are able to render judgment, not just on men's actions, but on their souls. Pessimism about humanity and about the future feeds the belief that the end of the world is just around the corner, while the belief in the rapidly approaching Tribulation makes such pessimism logical and necessary. Those who don't embrace this pessimism are viewed with suspicion, and if they claim to be Christian, they are often labeled "liberal" or charged with lacking "true knowledge of the Word."

Fundamentalism and dispensationalism are shot through with the conviction that "true believers" possess secret knowledge attainable only through their system of interpreting Scripture and rightly discerning "the signs of the times." They demand a radical distinction between Old Testament Israel and the Church, as well as an arrogant — even hostile — attitude toward the material world. Since the end is so near and this world is passing away, there's no need to invest time and effort in social, cultural, or political institutions and efforts.

[27] *Revelation Unveiled*, 66-67.

The Christian life should be oriented toward Heaven and eternity, free from the impediments of a depraved world.

All of these reasons — along with others — convinced me that the pretribulational Rapture is not a "blessed hope," as its proponents teach, but an unbiblical, false promise. The Second Coming is indeed our "blessed hope," for it is "the appearing of the glory of our great God and Savior, Christ Jesus."[28] God doesn't have two peoples, but one,[29] "for in Christ Jesus you are all sons of God, through faith. For as many of you as were baptized into Christ have put on Christ. There is neither Jew nor Greek, there is neither slave nor free, there is neither male nor female; for you are all one in Christ Jesus."[30]

A last-ditch attempt to steer me clear of Rome

One evening that winter, completely on impulse, I called Richard. I hadn't spoken with him for well over a year, and I didn't know what he had heard about our situation. Our conversation began quietly enough. I gave him a little background and told him we were probably going to enter the Catholic Church in the spring. Slowly his intensity level grew, and finally he began to attack the "Romanist" Church, with its needless "ritual and pomp" and its "unbiblical traditions and false teachings." He began to rail against the organization and hierarchy of the Church.

"You think the church is an organization, and it is not. It is spiritual and has no physical organization," he said. "Early

[28] Titus 2:13.
[29] Eph. 4:4-6.
[30] Gal. 3:26-28.

Christianity was simple. It didn't have organization and was never meant to have it."

"That's not what we find in the book of Acts and in the early Church Fathers," I replied.

He laughed. "Much of the early Church was in apostasy. Most of the early Church Fathers were apostates. Besides, their writings are not inspired and infallible."

"That's true," I replied, "but if I have to choose between fallible Church Fathers and fallible Reformers, I choose the Fathers."

He changed the subject. "The Roman Church has no authority," he said sharply. "The Bible is our authority. Scripture is absolutely authoritative and not to believe it is heresy."

"Can I read you something and get your thoughts on it?" I asked. He agreed.

I read 1 Timothy 3:15: "If I am delayed, you may know how one ought to behave in the household of God, which is the church of the living God, the pillar and bulwark of the truth."

There was a brief silence. "You're taking that out of context!" he exclaimed.

"How could I have taken it out of context? All I did was read a verse. I didn't even say what I thought it meant." The conversation went downhill from there. Richard called me heretical and told me that I was doing this only for attention.

"Why would I do it for this sort of attention?" I asked, "I can think of better types of attention."

"Well, you've always had a problem with your father and are using this to get at him," he claimed. Apparently he was referring to when I first met him and my father and I were in disagreement about the direction of my artwork.

"Becoming a Catholic is not a way to get back at someone," I replied. "The only reason I'm entering the Catholic Church is because it's true."

This angered him even more. "I'm surprised at how little you really know about the Evangelical faith," he said. "You've never really grasped the truths of Evangelicalism."

There were other revealing moments in our conversation. Richard asked me to explain why Catholics believe Jesus had no brothers or sisters when the Gospels mention His brothers and sisters.[31] "And don't try to tell me those are just the 'spiritual' brothers of Christ," he said.

I explained that the Greek word *adelphos*, used to describe these supposed siblings, is better translated as "close kinsmen," meaning these were likely cousins. When he scoffed at this, I pointed out that Protestant Greek dictionaries backed up my argument.

Irritated, Richard retorted, "That's the problem with Catholics — they never interpret the Bible literally!"

"If that's the case," I responded, "let's look at John 6 and Christ's demands that we eat His Flesh and drink His Blood."

He immediately claimed, once again, that I was taking words out of context, and never did explain to me what he thought Jesus meant by those shocking words. (Later that evening, I called Joel and told him about this part of my conversation with his father. As I explained why I thought the Catholic understanding of John 6 was true and irrefutable, Joel suddenly exclaimed, "That's crazy! What you are saying demands *too much faith*." I vividly recall how stunning this comment was to me. Here was a Protestant pastor claiming

---

[31] Matt. 12:47; Luke 8:19-20.

that there wasn't enough faith for him to believe what Jesus was saying.)

After three hours, my phone conversation with Richard was over. I had taken notes of everything he had said, and a few days later I wrote him a letter. "I don't want you to think that by questioning my motivation and sincerity, you have somehow proven the falsehood of Catholicism," I wrote. "Anyone who argues by attacking my motivation only convinces me of his own inability to answer the most difficult questions."

The six-page letter I received back from him was everything I expected it to be: harsh, condemning, polemical, and full of every anti-Catholic claim in the book: Catholics worship Mary, transubstantiation is stupid, Catholics aren't saved, the Church is in apostasy, the Pope is the Antichrist, and much more. It was packed with Scripture references, most of which were taken out of context. In concluding his letter, Richard urged Heather and me to return from our "spiritual defection" and return to the "truth."

Replying to the letter was a challenge I couldn't resist, even though I knew there was little chance of Richard's conceding any point, however obvious. My reply was forty pages long and contained nearly two hundred quotations from Scripture, the *Catechism*, and the works of Catholic theologians. In a few months, Richard would visit, in one last effort to "rescue" me from the errors of Rome. After another long and (to him) fruitless debate, he concluded, "I'm convinced you're not saved and never were."

Coming home to the kingdom

In the meantime, Heather and I continued to prepare for entering the Catholic Church. I didn't tell my parents what we were doing. They had become more and more upset, and for a while it was impossible to talk to them at all. Heather's parents were concerned, but they agreed to come and witness us enter the Church. At the Easter Vigil on March 29, 1997, we entered into full communion with the one, holy, catholic, and apostolic Church and received our Lord and Savior in the Eucharist. We had finally arrived home, by the grace of God.

Although we had lost some friends and our relationship with our families was strained, we had gained the Communion of Saints and the fullness of God's family, the Body of Christ.

Chesterton noted that it's an exciting adventure to explore and study the Catholic Church, but it's far easier than *being* a Catholic. He was certainly correct, but the excitement still remains. Every day is an adventure, a discovery of more riches and deeper grace as we make our pilgrimage here on earth.

From Christian Commune to Catholic Communion

I gave up everything I had in order to live
like the early Christians. Then I discovered
God's true plan for the Church.

Paul C. Fox, M.D.

On a muggy summer evening in 1991, I found myself
browsing restlessly through the religion section of the library of New College in Sarasota, Florida. My wife, Diane, and I had reached a momentous decision in the previous weeks: to quit our jobs (we were both family-practice physicians), sell all that we had, leave my aging parents, and take our four children to live in a Christian commune, which I'll simply call "the Community." There, we believed, we would live like the early Christians, having no property of our own, but placing ourselves fully at the service of "the church."

We had not reached this decision quickly or lightly. We had been aware of the Community for eight years and had made many visits — even living there for nearly a year — before we felt ready to make a final commitment. Yet even now, I felt an uneasiness in my heart. And being in the habit of seeking solace in books, I hoped that in the college library I would find one that would bring me relief, that would validate our decision and give me courage.

As my eyes scanned the faded, dusty spines of the books, they were caught by the single word: *Enthusiasm.* "Just what I need," I thought to myself. "More enthusiasm!"

I took Fr. Ronald Knox's classic work off the shelf and opened it to page 1. There I read:

> You have a clique, an elite, of Christian men and . . . women, who are trying to live a less worldly life than their neighbors; to be more attentive to the guidance . . . of the Holy Spirit. More and more, by a kind of fatality, you see them draw apart from their co-religionists, a hive ready to swarm. There is provocation on both sides; on the one part, cheap jokes at the expense of over-godliness, acts of stupid repression by unsympathetic authorities; on the other, contempt of the half-Christian, ominous references to old wine and new bottles, to the kernel and the husk. Then, while you hold your breath and turn away your eyes in fear, the break comes. . . . A fresh name has been added to the list of Christianities.

If Fr. Knox had deliberately set out to question the wisdom of our decision, he couldn't have done it more effectively than in that single paragraph. I knew that to read further would likely only increase my uneasiness; so, in one of the worst decisions I have ever made, I put *Enthusiasm* back on the shelf and tried to forget it.

Where is the one church?

That evening marked a fork in the spiritual road I had been traveling since the day Diane and I had come to believe in Christ twelve years earlier, when we were still medical students in Chicago. As new Christians, we had felt an urgent need to find "the church," for we believed almost instinctively that Christ had founded but one church and could not have allowed it to vanish from the earth — although we were prepared to believe it might be hidden.

But where, in the midst of all the competing "Christianities," was the church to be found? Since we had been raised in anti-Catholic environments, it did not even occur to us to examine the claims of the Catholic Church. We merely assumed — without any basis in fact — that such claims had long since been exploded by the Reformation.

Over the years, we passed through several churches and fellowships, finding ourselves drawn more and more to the radical witness of the sixteenth-century Anabaptists — forerunners of the present-day Mennonite denominations. We were attracted by their emphasis on simplicity and honesty, their insistence on the centrality of the Sermon on the Mount, their resolute stand against all violence, and their willingness to sacrifice everything, even their lives, for the sake of the gospel. Surely, we felt, the true New Testament church must be like them.

At that time, there was no Mennonite church where we lived. So in true Protestant style, we started one — a warm, close fellowship composed of members who took their Christianity seriously.

But from the beginning, even though the families in our church were like-minded for the most part, and even though we were content to call it "Mennonite," there was never any clear consensus on just what was meant by that designation or on how it should best be lived out. In fact, there was even a practicing Catholic couple in our group. They came simply because they loved the rest of us and enjoyed the fellowship. But they never for a moment relinquished their conviction that there was only one candidate for "the true church" — the Catholic Church. That a couple so obviously devoted to Christ could be so deluded (as we thought) was a disturbing puzzle.

Nor were they the only Catholic flies in our Anabaptist ointment. Somehow (I no longer remember how), we became subscribers to the *New Oxford Review (NOR)*, then an ecumenical journal of orthodox Christianity. In the pages of *NOR*, more than in any other Christian periodical, we found sound Christian thinking and doctrine. Yet most of the authors — especially the ones we liked best — were Catholic.

If this weren't enough, I had begun to read translations of the writings of the Christians who had been active in the first few centuries after Christ. After all, if we were seeking to find or re-invent the "New Testament Church," surely those who had lived closest in time to Christ and His Apostles would offer some helpful clues as to what such a church should look like. To my dismay, the "early Church" revealed in these writings seemed far more Catholic than Anabaptist.

In 1990 I finally decided to read a Catholic book about the Catholic Faith (instead of a Protestant book debunking the Faith): a mildewed and worm-eaten copy of Fr. Leo Trese's *The Faith Explained* that I discovered in a used bookstore for twenty-five cents.

I found it fascinating — and terrifying. If Fr. Trese couldn't fully persuade me of the truth of the Catholic Faith, at the very least he forced me to abandon any idea that Catholicism was completely contrary to Scripture and teeming with medieval superstitions and pagan remnants. On the contrary, I found myself thinking that it was not entirely inconceivable that I might one day become Catholic.

In spite of my newly acquired knowledge, the idea that I might "go over to the enemy" was frightening to me, and doubly so to Diane, who had not shared my interest in exploring Catholicism and feared that it might lead to a religious division between us.

Still, through my reading I had come to the conclusion that there were only two forms of Christianity that were consistent within themselves: classic Anabaptism and Catholicism. The two were as opposed to each other as two Christian faiths could be. One was congregational, the other hierarchical. One had merely symbolic "ordinances," the other supernaturally efficacious sacraments. One based itself with seeming immediacy on the New Testament; the other was grounded in a many-layered Tradition that included but was not limited to the Holy Scriptures.

Such was the fork in the road I had reached. Our fears and prejudices blocked the path leading to the Catholic Church. But where did the Anabaptist path lead?

Trying to live as the early Christians

At the same time that I had been exploring Catholicism, Diane and I had also been drawing ever closer to the Community. Here was a group that proudly claimed as its spiritual heritage the radical Anabaptist movement of the 1600s — a group that intentionally set out to revive the vision of those early Anabaptists. Indeed, like some of the most radical Anabaptists, its members had abolished all private property in order to live in full community of goods, basing themselves on Acts 4:32: "Now, the company of those who believed were of one heart and soul, and no one said that any of the things which he possessed was his own, but they had everything in common."

So in August 1991 we found ourselves driving into a beautiful green, wooded country in Appalachia, where we believed we were joining ourselves to Christ's true, New Testament church. There, we felt sure, we would find our heart's desire.

To a certain extent, we did find it. There, in the Community, we discovered the exhilarating sense of liberation that comes when one leaves the world and its daily cares behind. No more checkbook to balance. No need to shop for food and clothing. No need even to wonder what to wear from one day to the next: the Amish-style garb left little room for variety.

We left behind our future cares, too. No need to worry about malpractice suits, to save for retirement or for college, or to wonder whether we would spend our last days in a nursing home. The Community provided nurseries for the infants and toddlers, school for the children, and loving care for the elderly. Even the dying were surrounded by the love of community members: bouquets of wildflowers, drawings of angels by toddlers, and groups of schoolchildren singing at the bedside.

All is not perfect in the Community

Yet we also made unpleasant discoveries. We found, for one thing, that whereas the Community held equality of members to be a guiding principle, some members were more equal than others. If there were private music lessons or riding lessons for children, it was generally for the children of the Community's leaders. Where communal meals consisted of simple fare such as chicken and baked bologna, the leaders often enjoyed steak and lobster snacks during their daily meetings. We noticed that although radios, videos, and certain types of music were forbidden to ordinary members, you could still find them in the homes of the leaders.

This material inequality mirrored an inequality in power within the Community. Although the Community proclaimed that every important decision was made by the unanimous agreement of all baptized members, in reality the vast majority of decisions — particularly the most important ones — were made by the leaders of the Community and imposed upon the members. Often, this occurred with no discussion at all. When there was discussion, the leaders were adept at silencing any opposition.

The authority of the leaders converged in one man, whom I'll call "Frank." The overseer of the Community for many years, Frank possessed supreme power and unassailable opinions. It was Frank who gave the female members the freedom to wear colored head-scarves instead of black ones — then rebuked them for being "worldly" if they coordinated the color of their scarves to the color of their dresses. Frank often spoke of the witness of the Amish-style garb that we wore, yet he himself abandoned it in favor of a three-piece suit when attending a public meeting with other religious leaders. I can report without exaggeration that his authoritative opinions extended even to the proper way in which married couples were to make love, and whether you should use liquid or bar soap on your hands.

This form of leadership resulted directly from the Community's theology, with its emphasis on "the living Word." Instead of looking to "dead traditions," there was a reliance on the direct, day-to-day inspiration of the Holy Spirit, guiding the Community in the most minute details. And although the

Spirit might speak even through the humblest members, it was accepted that the gift of "discerning the Spirit" was given to the leaders — especially to Frank.

This approach led to erratic swings in the Community's beliefs and behavior, even during the short time we were members. As a simple example: at the time we joined, the Community (in common with other conservative Anabaptist groups) considered it worldly to vote in local or national elections. However, a few years into our time there, a local election affecting the Community's economic interests came up. Abruptly, it was not only permissible, but even a matter of "showing love for the brethren" to vote in that election — and to vote for a particular candidate.

This leadership by personal whim led the Community in some very strange directions indeed. Under Frank's leadership, this pacifist Anabaptist group found itself allied with the Nation of Islam and the Socialist Workers Party. We were exhorted to admire Louis Farrakhan as "another Martin Luther King." Frank himself traveled to Cuba and personally congratulated Fidel Castro on "all the good he has done for the Cuban people" (without a word about religious persecution) and sent a group of naïve women members on a trip to Iraq, from which they returned to report about the great love the Iraqi people have for Saddam Hussein.

It shouldn't be surprising that Frank's opinions about the Catholic Church were equally emphatic and ill-informed. The Catholic Church was, he told us, "terribly corrupt," and he equated the celebration of the Mass with magic. Although I had learned enough about Catholicism to know better, I lacked the courage to confront Frank about his misconceptions. After all, I had already been labeled a racist for pointing out the anti-Semitic, indeed anti-Christian, character of the Nation of Islam.

Not all members of the Community were as easily cowed. On one occasion, Frank was informing the community's members that if the Pope declared black to be white, Catholics were obliged to believe it, "because the Pope is infallible." An elderly member who had been a Catholic seminarian in his youth rose up in the meeting and very carefully explained that the doctrine of papal infallibility meant nothing of the kind. Frank merely commented that "things have changed in the Catholic Church since you were young" and continued in the same vein.

After five years of trying to justify to ourselves the behavior of the Community's leadership, we finally worked up the courage to bring our concerns to one of the ministers. His response was to place us immediately into "church discipline," forbidding us to speak to anyone but the leaders. A few weeks later, we found ourselves called to an extraordinary meeting of all the Community's members, with Frank himself presiding. We were accused of several counts of "betrayals" and were sentenced to expulsion from the Community until such time as we might "find repentance."

Thus, five years after driving into the Community, we drove out again, shorn both of the material assets we had accumulated before we joined and of the illusions that had led us there. During those years, amid much that was truly good and beautiful, we had also experienced firsthand the kinds of erratic, impulse-driven vagaries of belief and practice that characterize a movement that respects neither any living tradition nor the letter of the Scripture, but depends entirely on the ability of its human leaders to "discern the Spirit." In short, we lived the very things that Fr. Knox had vainly tried to warn us against in *Enthusiasm*.

Catholic Church or *no* church?

G. K. Chesterton once observed, "The moment men cease to pull against the Catholic Church, they feel a tug toward it." Anabaptism had exerted a powerful pull away from its diametrical opposite, the Catholic Church. At the moment of our expulsion from the Community, the pull of the Anabaptist pole was annihilated. There remained only one option: the Catholic Church.

Or rather, two options: the Catholic Church or no church.

How can there be Christianity with no church? Actually, this idea is implicit in the very spirit of Protestantism, particularly in its more radical forms. Anabaptism teaches that, in founding the church, Christ did not establish any identifiable or permanent institution. Instead, the church is simply the assembly of believers. Insofar as a group is made up of *true* believers, obedient to the Holy Spirit, it is the church. If such a group grows cold in its faith, no longer responsive to the Spirit, then it is no longer the church.

Mainstream Protestant denominations do not stress this "believers' church" ecclesiology as much as the Anabaptist groups do. Yet it remains implicit in Protestantism of all stripes. Without it, how could the Reformers have justified their break with the only church Western Christendom had known for 1500 years? Without it, how could later reformers justify breaking away from their parent churches to found new denominations?

I was beginning to see that this believers' church approach was inevitably subjective. After all, how does one determine that all members of a church are true believers? What are the evidences of true belief? Verbal confession of faith? Baptism as an adult? Abstinence from alcohol and tobacco? Wearing plain clothes? Driving a buggy instead of a car? During the twenty years I had been a Christian, I had accepted the believers'-church approach. Yet now I could see that in the years since the Reformation, this approach had led to the splintering of Protestantism, making it impossible to identify Christ's church with any certainty. Instead, one was confronted with a myriad of sects, each claiming to be a believers' church and each with its unique version of what to believe and how to act.

It wasn't easy for me to turn my back on an ecclesiology that had been part of my faith since I first accepted Christ. But I began to suspect that this couldn't have been Christ's plan when He founded the church.

Such was the state of my mind when I made the first entry in the journal I began in January 1997:

> The only valid reason for joining the Catholic Church would be *truth*. Is Catholic teaching more perfectly or completely true than that of other churches? Is the Catholic Church really *the* church in some way that other churches are not? If so, then as a Christian I should be Catholic.
>
> If not, then presumably Christ does not have a church on earth, in the sense of a definable institution. There are only "churches" that are "*the* church" only insofar as the believers are obedient to the Holy Spirit.
>
> Having become disenchanted with the believers'-church ideal, I am ready to entertain the alternative:

namely, that Christ in fact founded a visible and enduring church; and that despite its many faults, failings,
sins, and even crimes, the Roman Catholic Church just
may be it.

How I can reach any conclusion on this question, I
don't know. I will just read the *Catechism*, write down
my thoughts and questions, ponder, ask, and pray for
God's leading.

With this resolve, I began my exploration of that wonderful gift to the Church and the world, the *Catechism of the Catholic Church*.

It was not long before I found a passage that seemed like a
welcome mat laid at the door of the Church: "Our holy
mother the Church holds and teaches that God, the first principle and last end of all things, can be known with certainty by
the natural light of human reason. Without this capacity, man
would not be able to welcome God's revelation. Man has this
capacity because he is created 'in the image of God.' "[32]

It can be imagined that the reference to "our holy mother
the Church" caused a great deal of unease in my Protestant
soul. Still, the rest of the statement struck me as being both
very Catholic (for I had certainly never heard it expressed in
any Protestant church) and very true. It had a bracing effect
on me. As I wrote then:

I am encouraged by this statement. I have spent the
last five years in an environment in which reason is not
welcome. Yet the reasoning process is so much a part of
my makeup that it is very heartening to see it affirmed.

[32] CCC, par. 36.

Everybody has a tradition

Thus set free to reason, I began to reason my way out of the Protestant mindset into the mind of the Church. The first item I dealt with was the Church's teaching concerning Scripture and Tradition. It was no secret that the Catholic Church does not base her teachings on "Scripture alone," as Protestant churches claim to do. The early Anabaptists in particular were biblicists par excellence, even denouncing Luther himself for relying too much on Tradition!

Yet, as I thought about it, I began to see that every denomination has some extrabiblical tradition by which it interprets Scripture (although most will deny it). These traditions yield a clear, hard-edged teaching about issues on which Scripture is ambiguous.

The Mennonites, for example, reject the baptism of infants and are strict pacifists. Yet although it is possible to make a case for both positions from Scripture, you can make an equally strong biblical case (as other Protestant denominations do) for the contrary positions. To decide the issues, the Mennonites step outside the Bible and appeal to the practice of the early Church and the writings of the Apostolic Fathers, as well as to the faith and practice of the early Anabaptists and their descendants.

Every denomination also takes positions that are based, not on Scripture alone, but on an interpretation of Scripture that it considers authoritative. The Reformed churches have the tradition of Calvin; the Methodists, that of Wesley; "the Community," that of its founder.

Once I had recognized this point, the issue was no longer one of "*sola Scriptura* vs. Tradition." Rather, it became a question of which tradition, if any, I would accept as authoritative.

As I reflected on the competing claims of the various traditions, I wrote in my journal:

> The Catholic Tradition has this in support of its claim to authority: that for many centuries it was the *only* tradition and that during those centuries it defined and defended the doctrine which is the core belief of every Christian denomination: the Trinity. Explicitly or implicitly, *every* Christian denomination accepts as fully authoritative the decisions of the early Ecumenical Councils with regard to the Trinity.

Scripture alone doesn't give you the Trinity

It occurred to me that unquestioning acceptance of the doctrine of the Trinity was a serious problem for Anabaptist churches — indeed, for any church claiming to base its beliefs solely on Scripture. For the Bible simply doesn't provide a direct, unambiguous teaching about the Trinity. In fact, the Arians of the fourth century, like the Jehovah's Witnesses of today, were particularly adept at attacking Trinitarian doctrine by quoting reams of Scripture.

The doctrine of the Trinity was firmly established, not by reliance on Scripture alone, but by the authoritative decisions of the early Church councils. Yet these councils were the products of what Anabaptists (and many biblicist denominations) would consider an already "fallen" church, one that was everything the Anabaptists were not: hierarchical, liturgical, and sacramental. It was a church that baptized infants and justified wars. Why, I wondered, should Anabaptists cling to the doctrine of the Trinity, since it is the product of this "apostate church"?

Reflecting on this anomaly, I wrote:

I think the answer must be that there is a deep in-stinct, a warning signal implanted by the Holy Spirit, that says, "reject the Trinity and you will have left Christianity forever."

But the question remains: If the Spirit could give to all Christians a dogma of such overwhelming impor-tance through the councils of a "fallen" church, isn't it possible, or even likely, that the same church remains His chosen instrument for guiding Christians?

Anyone reading these paragraphs might conclude that they were the words of a Catholic apologist. In a sense, they were. At some point in my seeking — perhaps as I was turning the brittle pages of Fr. Trese's book in Sarasota — a "Catholic self" had been born in me. After being suppressed for half a dozen years, that Catholic self was now laboring mightily to overcome the resistance of the Protestant-Anabaptist self that had solidified over decades.

Having scored an important victory in the issue of *sola Scriptura*, my Catholic self had little trouble persuading me to accept the full canon of Scripture, as preserved by the Church. What a wonderful gift to have restored to my Bible all those "extra" books that had been so ruthlessly excised by the Reformers!

Is baptizing babies bad?

The question of infant Baptism, however, was a greater challenge. After all, only a dozen years before, I had persuaded myself, and fervently believed, that Baptism was for believing adults only and that it was unbiblical and even irrational to baptize infants, who had no capacity to believe. Was I now to reverse my thinking?

Here again I found that the Bible didn't yield a direct answer. To be sure, there is no explicit command to baptize infants. But there is also no prohibition. Moreover, there are tantalizing references to the baptism of whole households.

The Anabaptists had a simple explanation for the development of infant Baptism: it was the result of the "state takeover" of the Church under Constantine. After Christianity became the state religion, infant Baptism was introduced to ensure that all citizens would be members of the state church. But "New Testament baptism" was always confined to adult believers.

The chief problem with this explanation is that it's false. As I looked into the history of Baptism, I discovered unequivocal references to infant Baptism in second-century Christian writings — a good hundred years before Constantine, and at a time when Christianity was still under heavy attack from the state.

So infant Baptism was not, after all, the product of a "fallen" Church — unless one were ready to claim that the "fall" of the Church occurred within a generation after the death of the Apostles.

Still, "believers' baptism" had a very strong emotional hold on me. So strong, in fact, that I had been baptized *twice* as an adult (the second time just in case I hadn't believed sincerely enough the first time). It seemed so obviously right, and so very spiritual. As I wrote in March 1997:

> Now, personally I find — still! — that adult Baptism on confession of faith "makes more sense" than

infant Baptism. To my mind, the idea of "ordinances" seems rational, while the concept of "sacraments" seems rather spooky.

But I also find it pretty hard to accept that the Apostles did such a poor job of transmitting Christ's teachings that their immediate followers were already in grievous error about Baptism. For one thing, that would imply that the testimony of the early Church after the New Testament is completely unreliable as a guide to Christian faith and practice. If the early Christians could go so far astray so early on so important an issue, how could they be right about anything?

This has the further implication that Christianity must be ahistorical: that is, far from there being any continuity of faith and practice, each generation — even each individual believer — must rediscover and re-invent the "New Testament Church" based solely on the New Testament and guided by the Holy Spirit.

This is precisely what Protestantism has been attempting for five hundred years — and look where it has brought us! Will the real "New Testament Church" please stand up?

Really His Body, really His Blood

Although not mentioned in my journal for nearly four months, the question of the Church's teaching on the Eucharist — particularly the doctrine of transubstantiation[33] — was

---

[33] Through the consecration of the bread and the wine there occurs the change of the entire substance of the bread into the substance of the Body of Christ, and of the entire substance of the wine into the Blood of Christ — even though

never far from my mind. On the contrary, it loomed before me like a gigantic barricade, whose top I couldn't even see. As I tried to make sense of such phrases as "changing in substance while preserving the accidents," I despaired of ever being able to come to grips with the doctrine. And I knew that without unreservedly embracing the Church's teaching on this crucial issue, I could never honestly enter the Catholic Church.

Then it occurred to me that perhaps I was approaching the question from the wrong end. The doctrine of transubstantiation was the result of centuries of reflection, an attempt to put into words what is, in the end, not fully explicable — a mystery, in short. As with the doctrine of the Trinity, there was no question of a full understanding of the mystery, but only a question of whether the doctrine reflected, however imperfectly, something real.

So in April 1997 I found myself writing:

> The question should not be "What does the doctrine of transubstantiation mean, and do I agree with it?" but "What did Christ mean when He instituted the Eucharist?" This is a question that can be answered by referring to His own words and to the interpretation of them by His earliest disciples, i.e., the New Testament and the Apostolic Fathers. Having answered this question, "transubstantiation" will be recognized as either in harmony with this understanding of the Eucharist or not.

Turning first to the New Testament, I found, as with the doctrine of the Trinity, that there is no explicit statement that

the appearances of bread and wine remain. See CCC, par. 1376.

would establish Transubstantiation beyond any question; no passage that says baldly, "The bread and wine are changed into the Body and Blood of Christ." On the other hand, there are New Testament passages that seem to *imply* such a transformation. Jesus' words at the Last Supper — "This is my Body. This is my Blood" — could be interpreted that way. St. Paul's stern warning about "profaning the Body and Blood of the Lord"[34] is also particularly suggestive, for if the bread and wine are only symbols, how can one be guilty of profaning Christ Himself by taking them unworthily?

However, it was the words of Christ Himself in John 6 that struck the deepest chord: "He who eats my Flesh and drinks my Blood has eternal life . . . for my Flesh is food indeed and my Blood is drink indeed."[35] Meditating on this remarkable chapter of the Gospel, I wrote:

Strange that I never heard these words in the Protestant churches I grew up in! And somehow I managed not to notice them in my Bible reading for years afterward. When I finally did hear them, I was as offended by them as were the Jewish disciples who left Jesus on account of them, and I scrambled to find a "spiritual" interpretation to cover the offense.

To be sure, it's possible to put a spiritual spin on the words — everything Jesus did or said had spiritual meaning! But if these words were merely spiritual, if the eating of His Body and drinking of His Blood were merely symbolic, why didn't He say so? Why did He let so many souls turn from Him to perdition, if He could have

---

[34] 1 Cor. 11:28-29.
[35] John 6:54-55.

saved them by simply explaining away His shocking words? Perhaps because He meant exactly what He said!

In this way, I came to realize that the New Testament, if read without Protestant preconceptions, at least raised the possibility that the elements of the Eucharist really *are* the Body and Blood of Christ in some way that is much more than symbolic. If they are, they must *become* so during the celebration of the Eucharist, since they were certainly ordinary bread and wine beforehand. To say this much is to proclaim, in very simple terms, the doctrine of transubstantiation.

I didn't come to these insights unaided. After all, I had read Fr. Trese's book years before, and I was now reading the *Catechism*, along with a number of other books explaining and defending the Catholic Faith. But the sense of discovery — even using maps others had drawn and treading paths others had cleared — was still heady and intense.

A first-century apostasy?

Turning to the testimony of the early Church, I reviewed for myself what Ignatius of Antioch, Justin Martyr,[36] and others had to say about the Eucharist and found in them a uniform testimony that the bread and wine become the Body and Blood of Christ in the Eucharist — not symbolically, but actually. And since there is no substantial historical gap between the last writings of the New Testament and the oldest writings of the Apostolic Fathers, I had to accept their testimony as the strongest possible witness to what Christ actually intended when He instituted the Eucharist.

[36] St. Justin (d. c. 165), Christian apologist, writer, and martyr.

With this, the seemingly insurmountable barricade was ready to be scaled. The final triumph of my "Catholic self" resounds in what I wrote next:

> All that the doctrine of transubstantiation does is to make it very explicit that *change* means "change" and is not to be understood metaphorically. If night changes into day, it means that night is gone and day has taken its place. In the same way, if the bread and wine are changed into the Body and Blood of Christ, it means that the bread and wine are gone and the Body and Blood of Christ are there.
>
> In the end, though, it doesn't matter in the least whether or not I fully understand the doctrine of transubstantiation as stated by the Council of Trent in 1566. Trent was very clearly in harmony with the faith of the New Testament and the early Church.

This made the issue very clear: denial of the Real Presence, in the explicit form expressed by the doctrine of transubstantiation, presumes that the New Testament Church itself totally perverted the teaching of the Apostles. Still worse, it presumes that the early Christians universally fell into idolatry even during the lifetime of the Apostles — or that the Apostles themselves had utterly misconstrued the words of Jesus.

A non-Christian might accept such a proposition. But can a Christian believe that the Church fell into grievous error before the ink was dry on the last pages of the New Testament? Can we believe that such a fallen Church was able to hand on to us an infallible New Testament, or come to correct conclusions about the Trinity?

I could not.

I discover the Eastern Liturgy

In the spring of 1997, I began to take instruction in the Faith from Fr. Jacques Daley, of St. Vincent's Archabbey in Latrobe, Pennsylvania, where we now live. After a few conversations with me, Fr. Jacques remarked dryly, "I actually think you've been a Catholic for years!"

Perhaps. Still, it took nearly another year's worth of conversations with him to bring me to full acceptance of the Church's teachings. With gentleness and humor, Fr. Jacques corrected my misunderstandings, amplified my understanding, and prepared me to enter the Church, not as an enthusiast entering yet another sect, but as one more sinner whom Christ died to save, and to whom, in His incomprehensible humility, He was prepared to offer Himself as food "for the healing of soul and body."

Fr. Jacques also introduced me to the Byzantine Rite of the Catholic Church, for which I will be forever grateful to him. Somehow he sensed that the Liturgy and spirituality of Eastern Catholicism would be congenial to me.

It was on December 20, 1997 that Fr. Jacques took me to the Saturday evening Liturgy at St. Mary's Byzantine Catholic Church. He deposited me in a pew and disappeared behind the icon screen. I sat quietly, taking in the soft light of the chandeliers on the icons, breathing the heady aroma of incense, and drinking in the profoundly theological words of the Liturgy of St. John Chrysostom,[37] with its emphasis on the Holy Trinity "one in substance and undivided" and its recurrent refrain, "Lord have mercy!"

---

[37] St. John Chrysostom (c. 347-407), Archbishop of Constantinople and Doctor; named Chrysostom, or "Golden Mouth" for his eloquent preaching.

I wrote in my journal the next day:

I had the strongest feeling of joy, and of homecoming. It seemed that after years — almost two decades — of seeking, I had found what I had been looking for: *worship*.

I knew that I had found my particular home within the universal Church.

The last entry in my journal reads:

On May 2, 1998, the Feast of St. Athanasius,[38] I was received into the Catholic Church by chrismation[39] at St. Mary's Byzantine Catholic Church, Bradenville, Pennsylvania, and received the Blessed Sacrament, the Body and Blood of Christ, at the hand of my sponsor and spiritual guide, Fr. Jacques Daley, O.S.B.

No longer the only Catholic in the family

Diane's reaction throughout this process ranged from resistance, and even anger, to gradual acceptance. By the time I was received into the Church, she had come to understand that this was a step I needed to take if I was to be faithful to my conscience. On Easter in 1998, she gave me a Ukrainian Easter egg that she had painstakingly decorated herself, prominently featuring a Byzantine cross. It was her way of saying, "Go ahead, with my blessing." Still, it seemed at the time that I was likely to remain the only Catholic in the family.

---

[38] St. Athanasius (c. 297-373), Bishop of Alexandria and Doctor.

[39] *Chrismation* is a common Eastern Christian term for the sacrament of Confirmation. It is derived from the sacred oil, or chrism, used in the Confirmation rite.

But Diane came with me to Mass every Saturday evening (I attended the Mennonite services with her on Sundays), and little by little, the beauty and profundity of the divine Liturgy began to speak to her. She quietly did her own reading and praying, asked her own questions, struggled through her own difficulties, and spoke with Fr. Jacques and with our parish priest. After a year, to my surprise and great joy, Diane entered the Church, and we both had the joy of seeing our twelve-year-old daughter, Elizabeth, baptized and chrismated during the same Liturgy.

It has now been four years since I was received into the Church — four years that have brought many blessings. The divine Liturgy and the incalculable privilege of receiving Christ in the Eucharist remain the central point of my faith — at once the goal of each week and the place where each succeeding week begins anew.

True, some of my Evangelical friends believe I have lost my mind, and some may even believe I have lost my salvation (for some, "assurance of salvation" apparently doesn't apply to converts to Catholicism). But God has introduced us to new friends: fervent Catholics who love the Lord and His Church, and friends who have gone before us into the Church Triumphant: the saints and Doctors of the Church, who have so much to teach us and whose prayers are so powerful with God.

In the Catholic Church, Christ has indeed built "a house of many mansions"[40] and continues to build it. We have barely crossed the threshold of that marvelous royal palace. We look forward to years — to an eternity! — of exploring the beautiful rooms He has so lovingly prepared for us.

[40] Cf. John 14:2.

Lookin' for Truth
in All the Wrong Places

*I searched everywhere for a convincing refutation
of Catholicism, but the harder I looked, the more
I discovered that I should become Catholic.*

Pam Forrester

When I was eight, I asked my mom to take me to the little church at the end of our street. She began to drop me off every week for Sunday school. One Sunday, my teacher presented the Gospel and encouraged us to accept Jesus Christ as our Savior.

"But," she told us, "you must be willing to do anything for God, such as becoming a missionary."

Well, I really wanted to be saved, but I did *not* want to be a missionary! I had to think this over. I went home and thought about it for a while, my little eight-year-old soul struggling against selfish desire. Several weeks later, I convinced myself that I'd be willing to be a missionary for Jesus, and I asked Him to come into my heart.

For years I had a very fervent faith, even up to my first year in college — when the theory of evolution and the desire to sin enticed me to abandon my faith. I conveniently became an atheist for two years during the '60s. Then my mom gave me a copy of *The Late Great Planet Earth*, a book about the Second

Coming of Christ. After reading it, I decided that perhaps the Bible *was* relevant after all and not just some dusty old book I could safely ignore.

So I rededicated my life to Christ. I gave a copy of *The Late Great Planet Earth* to my boyfriend, Mike, a first-year medical student, and he committed his life to Christ, too. A year later, we took a Bible course called the Bethel Series — a two-year overview of the whole Bible. We got married, taught the Bethel Series, led small-group Bible studies, and studied Scripture in depth. We moved from California to Baltimore so that Mike could do his surgery residency at Johns Hopkins Hospital. Then we moved to Houston so he could do specialty training.

Scripture study leads us to unpopular conclusions

Since we were convinced that the Bible alone was sufficient for faith and salvation, we wanted to know exactly what the words in the Bible meant. I bought a Greek dictionary and a Greek interlinear Bible and taught myself to read the Greek alphabet. When Mike finished his residency, we moved to California with our three young children. Mike set up practice in a small town north of San Diego. We found a great church, and we joined a weekly Bible-study group.

It was here that we first heard about the doctrine of Eternal Security — the belief that once a Christian is "saved," he can't lose salvation, no matter what he does. We objected initially, but were assured that this doctrine was true, our friends firing off memorized Bible verses to support it. We backed down for a while. Then Mike began his own Bible study by listening to tapes of the Bible while exercising. I also studied, on my own, with my dictionaries, concordances, and Greek interlinear. Before long, Mike was using these sources as well. We soon became convinced that there were hundreds of verses that didn't align with the "once saved, always saved" doctrine. Our Bible-study group swelled to overflowing as Mike taught how Scripture refuted Eternal Security. We were labeled Arminian, although we had never heard of Arminius[41] or what he wrote. But we did reject Calvinism, especially the doctrine of Limited Atonement.[42]

Our pastors didn't agree with us, but since everything Mike was teaching was biblical, he was allowed to continue as an elder in the church and even to teach from the pulpit several times a year. Some people agreed with us; some were convinced we were heretics, and told us so. Mike's sermons usually caused controversy. The board of elders tried to talk Mike out of speaking on Eternal Security issues; others tried to show us the error of our ways.

We feared for the souls of those who might think they were eternally secure and bound for Heaven, no matter what kind of life they lived. Mike even wrote a two-volume book and was asked to teach at a Bible college by a popular radio preacher in order to point out the errors of the "once saved, always saved" theology.

We were still convinced that once all the biblical evidence was compiled, it would be irresistibly persuasive and all our friends and pastors would see the truth.

[41] Early seventeenth-century Dutch theologian who rejected, among other things, the Calvinist doctrine of predestination.

[42] Core Calvinist teaching that the effects of Christ's Redemption are meant for a limited group of "elect," not for the whole world.

But the evidence was met with a yawn. Those who disagreed with us didn't refute the scriptural evidence — they just ignored it. We were astounded! We eventually realized that most people didn't really practice *sola Scriptura* after all; they clung to the Protestant traditions begun by Luther and Calvin, sometimes in spite of Scripture. After ten years of attempting to show how the Bible doesn't support Eternal Security, being called heretics, and hearing through the grapevine about people who resented and suspected us, we became discouraged and disillusioned.

If I hadn't been so thoroughly convinced there was a God, I could easily have become an atheist. In my heart, I was prideful, arrogant, and critical. No church quite suited me, since most Protestant churches incorporate some form of Calvinism. According to *my* understanding of the Bible, which I was convinced was led by the Holy Spirit, all the nearby churches were wrong about something. Despite this, I sensed that my attitude wasn't Christlike, so I would pray about that. I wanted to be humble, but I just wasn't. "Maybe I am a heretic," I thought. "What makes me so sure I'm right and other Christians are wrong?" I desperately wanted to find a church in which I could simply worship God without being critical. In the meantime, all I could do was studiously try to keep my mind from dwelling on criticisms. I thought I could be content in my apathy.

Not so weird after all?

A few years later, in the summer of 1997, while perusing home-school curriculum catalogs, I saw a course for junior-high-school students designed to introduce Protestants to the Catholic Faith and vice versa. The student was supposed to read the books in one order if he was Protestant and in the opposite order if he was Catholic, so that the last book read confirmed him in his own faith tradition. Since my oldest daughter had just started attending a Catholic university, I decided that this would be the perfect time to find out more about the Catholic Faith. That way, if Heather came home with questions, I'd be able to answer them. *But I didn't want her to become Catholic!*

I ordered three books. The first, *Evangelical Is Not Enough*, was written by Thomas Howard, a convert to Catholicism and the brother of prominent Evangelical Elizabeth Elliot. I had long been curious about why a Christian would join the Catholic Church and found Howard's story interesting. Howard made a lot of sense, and I grew slightly annoyed that I had accepted so many misconceptions about the Catholic Faith. "Hey," I thought, "maybe the Catholic Church isn't so weird after all."

One evening at our Bible study, my husband brought up John 14:26, where Jesus says, "The Holy Spirit, whom the Father will send in my name, He will teach you all things, and bring to your remembrance all that I have said to you." Mike reminded everyone that our usual interpretation of this verse was that this promise was given to each and every believer. The result has been that there are now more than twenty-five thousand Protestant denominations. But the Catholic view, as Howard had explained it, is that this promise was made in the upper room to the Twelve Apostles, and thus it applied only to them and to their successors: the Pope and the Catholic leaders. Without the final, ruling authority of Christ through the Bishop of Rome and the Magisterium, the Catholic Church would splinter into even more sects than in Protestantism.

I was aghast, because I wasn't ready to say anything yet. No one said much, and we went on with the study as usual. But I found out the next day that one of my best friends at the study had cried all the way home. She had been shocked to hear us say something outside of "Scripture alone." And I didn't blame her. I decided then not to say a word to anyone about my research into the Catholic Church until it became absolutely necessary, if ever.

After reading Howard's book, I felt very broadminded toward the Catholic Church. But I didn't sense the danger to my Protestantism as I opened up the second book: *Catholicism and Fundamentalism*, by Karl Keating. This book promised Catholic answers to the charges against "Romanism" by "Bible Christians." By the time I had read about half of the book, I felt no longer broadminded, but sick and horrified all at once. I had read enough of Keating's book to learn, for the first time, that Catholicism had a defense for beliefs such as the Eucharist and the papacy. Keating's use of Scripture was standard exegesis. It made sense. What I read in that book coalesced with doubts and questions I had put on the back burners of my mind. No longer simmering, they began to boil.

For instance, I had long wondered how each and every individual person's faith could rest on personal devotional Bible reading, when most people, until relatively modern times, couldn't even read. And even if they could read, most people wouldn't be able to own a Bible because Bibles were hand-copied (until the sixteenth century) and were very expensive.

Personal devotional Bible reading for growing in Christ began to seem suspiciously modern — especially when I discovered that the Catholic Church had read Scripture to the faithful at every Mass for two thousand years. But could the

Catholic Church be the one Church founded by Jesus Christ Himself?

No! Never! It couldn't possibly be true.

My soul in turmoil, I slammed *Catholicism and Fundamentalism* shut and grabbed the book that was supposed to confirm me in my Protestant faith, *The Gospel According to Rome*, by James McCarthy.

Looking for Protestant answers from the early Christians

In McCarthy's book, I was looking for a rebuttal to Catholic Scripture interpretation. I wanted to know why Jesus didn't *literally* mean to eat His Flesh in John 6, when that sure seemed like what He said. I wanted to know exactly why Jesus didn't found His Church on Peter in Matthew 16, when that is what He said. I wanted to know what was wrong with confession to a priest when the Bible says, "confess your sins to one another,"[43] and "Receive the Holy Spirit. . . . Whose sins you forgive, they are forgiven. . . ."[44]

But *The Gospel According to Rome* didn't help at all. It didn't address my questions, but merely explained why Catholicism was wrong according to traditional Protestant *interpretations* of certain biblical passages. It never convincingly refuted the Catholic interpretation of verses that supported Catholic beliefs.

Now I really felt scared. I begged God to show me the truth about what was wrong with the Catholic Church. I didn't want to be Catholic. There were no Catholics in either of our

[43] James 5:16.
[44] John 20:22-23.

families. I had never been anti-Catholic; I believed there were a few real Christians in the Catholic Church in spite of Catholicism. I liked Catholics. I just didn't want to *be* one!

I stopped reading for several weeks. I needed to get my perspective back. I thought and prayed. When I felt calm again, I picked up Keating's book and finished it. Yes, the Catholic Church had good reasons, biblical reasons, for her theology. But I was certain there had to be a good Protestant refutation, by somebody, somewhere.

But here was my dilemma. We had this early Church that we trusted to tell us which writings floating around the ancient world were inerrant and inspired. It seemed logical, then, that we should be able to trust this same Church and the doctrines taught by it at least up until the time the Bible was canonized. Right? We always used to talk about the Church of the Apostles and how it was the true model for Christian belief and practice. So, when reading the Acts of the Apostles, we sought to align our present-day worship with what we found in sacred Scripture. Seeking to worship in imitation of the early Church was a foundational principle. Therefore, you can imagine my shock when I discovered that this early Church believed in that particularly Catholic doctrine, the Real Presence of Christ in the Eucharist.

> "They abstain from the Eucharist and from prayer, because they do not confess that the Eucharist is the Flesh of our Savior Jesus Christ, Flesh which suffered for our sins and which the Father, in His goodness, raised up again." — *St. Ignatius of Antioch*

> "We call this food *Eucharist*; and no one else is permitted to partake of it, except one who believes. . . . So

too, as we have been taught, the food which has been made into the Eucharist by the eucharistic prayer set down by Him, and by the change of which our blood and flesh is nourished, is both the Flesh and the Blood of that incarnated Jesus." — *St. Justin*

Jesus tells His followers *eight* times to eat His Flesh in John 6. I came to the inescapable conclusion that the earliest Christians took Jesus literally. When I found out that even Martin Luther — one of the principal fathers of the Reformation — believed in the Real Presence, I realized that Christians had always believed this doctrine.

Can anything good come out of a corrupted Church?

This put me in a tough position.

On the one hand, the early Church canonized the Bible around the year 400. On the other hand, that very same early Church believed in the Real Presence of Christ (and, I was discovering, many other Catholic doctrines). The standard Protestant solution to this dilemma was that these strange Catholic doctrines were pagan corruptions of the pure and simple Christianity of the Apostles. But I could no more take the Bible from the hand of a church that was supposed to be corrupted by paganism than I could accept the *Pearl of Great Price* (an extrabiblical text considered part of inspired Scripture by Mormons) while rejecting everything else about the Mormon belief system. That seemed totally irrational. I couldn't buy it.

Being a Protestant was like watching a Corpus Christi procession, then rushing up and knocking down the priests and nuns, candles, censors, crucifix, and monstrance, but grabbing the Bible and carrying it away and basing faith on it alone. What sense does that make? I just couldn't find a logical way to accept the authority of the Bible while rejecting the beliefs of the very earliest Christian Church, which, under the guidance of the Holy Spirit (which we must believe) chose the books that make up the Bible.

"Come back! I'm just being symbolic!"

I began to read Catholic books, hoping to find the Church's Achilles heel.

Nothing.

Still resisting, I called Hector, a pastor friend who had a ministry to bring Hispanics out of the Catholic Church. He seemed likely to know the intricacies of Catholic doctrine and what was wrong with it. I told him what I was going through, and he sympathetically recommended *The Gospel According to Rome*. I told him I had read it and it wasn't convincing.

Then he asked, "But, what about the fact that Jesus had brothers? The Bible talks about the brothers and sisters of Jesus."

My experience with Greek had already helped me tackle this question.

"I looked that up, and the Greek word can legitimately be translated 'kinsman' or 'brother' depending upon the context," I said. "That same Greek word is translated 'kinsman' in lots of other places in the New Testament. So the Catholics could be right about Mary's being ever-virgin," I said.

He kindly promised to pray for me, and we hung up. I stared into space and wondered, "Is that the best he can do?"

A few hours later, my pastor called. I figured Hector must have called him, so I told him all about my dilemma. Then I asked, "Why don't we believe in the Real Presence of Christ in Communion when Jesus says in John 6 over and over that we must eat His Body and drink His Blood in order to have eternal life? Why don't we take it literally, as Catholics do?"

"That is just symbolic," he responded, "because later Jesus says the flesh is of no avail."

"Yes, Jesus says, 'The flesh is of no avail,' but what does He *mean* by that? Jesus is God in the flesh. Is His Flesh of no avail?"

"Well of course *His* Flesh is important. The 'flesh of Jesus availeth much.' But Jesus is speaking symbolically when He talks about *eating* His Flesh."

"But how do we *know* that for certain?" I asked.

"Because the Old Testament strictly forbids cannibalism."

"You're right. But the Old Testament prohibition against cannibalism is exactly why many of Jesus' Jewish disciples left Him at this point saying, 'This is a hard saying; who can listen to it?' And as far as we know, Jesus didn't chase after them and say, 'Wait, I was only speaking symbolically!' So the disciples who left understood Jesus to be speaking literally. Otherwise, why would they leave? So somehow Jesus must have been speaking literally and yet not advocating cannibalism. The Catholic doctrine of the Eucharist is literal and yet not literally cannibalistic, since Jesus didn't cut off His arm and pass it around saying, 'Take, eat.' How can we as Protestants respond to this?"

He mumbled some kind of answer that made no impression; then he changed the subject, asking, "Well, what about all the money they spent building cathedrals when people were starving?"

"But when they built a cathedral, it was like a giant welfare project. People had work for years and years," I replied.

He changed the subject again: "The Catholic Church became corrupted by pagan beliefs shortly after the Apostles died."

"Well, then, wouldn't that mean that the gates of Hell prevailed against His Church and Jesus was unable to keep that promise?"[45]

"No, there was always a remnant."

"But how can we know for sure that the remnant part of the Church, the true Church of Christ, was the one that canonized the Bible and not the corrupted part of the Church?"

"We just trust that the Holy Spirit was able to do that."

"But the earliest Christians held Catholic beliefs such as the Real Presence of Jesus in the Eucharist and the perpetual virginity of Mary. Who threw these beliefs out? Luther believed them. Luther and Calvin believed Mary was a perpetual virgin. Who decided Mary definitely had other children when everyone right up to and including the Reformation believed she gave birth only to Jesus?"

Our conversation continued like this for several hours. When my pastor couldn't give an answer, he changed the subject. I wasn't actually defending the Church at that point. I was telling him the Catholic viewpoint in desperate hope that he could give me a convincing Protestant rebuttal. But nothing he said was convincing.

Later I wrote him letters with about forty questions and included a review of the books I had read. He was in a doctoral program, and I hoped he could get some answers from his professors. When we talked again, he said I had done so much research that he didn't have time to get up to speed with me. He

---

[45] Cf. Matt. 16:18.

told me to go ahead and visit a Catholic Church, thinking that would put an end to my fantasy. Meanwhile I kept searching for a Protestant refutation of the Catholic Faith. There just *had* to be one.

Mary needed a savior, too

Next, I watched a video debate between Jesuit Fr. Mitch Pacwa and two prominent Protestant apologists (Walter Martin and John Ankerberg). Again, there was no refutation of Catholic claims, no explanation of what was wrong with Catholic exegesis — only what was wrong with Catholic beliefs, according to the interpretation of Scripture in a particular Protestant tradition. My husband, who was at once fascinated by the Catholic interpretation of Sacred Scripture and at the same time repulsed by the thought of becoming Catholic, was also disappointed that no one refuted the points Fr. Pacwa made. Martin and Ankerberg never explained why Fr. Pacwa's interpretation was wrong. They merely condemned Catholic theology according to what they thought the Bible meant.

For example, I remember Martin asking, "Why does the Catholic Church believe Mary was without sin when she admits that God is her Savior in Luke 1:47? She must have needed a Savior because she sinned."

Fr. Pacwa replied, "Yes, she needed a Savior. But a person can be saved out of a pit after he has fallen in, or he can be saved from the pit before he falls in. We believe God saved Mary *before* she fell into sin by creating her, from conception, without the fallen nature caused by the stain of Original Sin, which she otherwise would have inherited from her parents. So He created Mary without sin, just as He created Adam and Eve without sin."

Martin and Ankerberg would then go on to another topic without dealing with Fr. Pacwa's explanations.

My ex-Catholic friends are of no help

I decided to find out why some of my ex-Catholic friends had left the Church. One of them, I was surprised to learn, was on the verge of returning to the Catholic Church. The others had just drifted away when their parents could no longer make them go to Sunday Mass. None had left for any particular doctrinal reason.

One friend of my mother-in-law assured me the Catholic Church was really weird and unscriptural because she remembered, as a young, devout Catholic, having to go from church to church all in one day in order to say prayers for her loved ones. She assured me that she couldn't pray for all the people she cared about in one church, but was allowed to pray for only one person per church. I have since asked priests and lay-Catholic friends whether they've ever heard of this; none have. Perhaps my mother-in-law's friend misunderstood or was misinformed. Even if it were true, it seems to me little reason to reject the Church!

A professional anti-Catholic takes his best shot

After six months of frantic detective work, I had exhausted every avenue I could think of to find a Protestant rebuttal to Catholic doctrine. There were, of course, many great Protestant arguments out there. The trouble with them was that they rebutted doctrines that Catholics didn't believe. For instance, you could find lots of apologetic material condemning the worship of Mary, complete with Scriptures against idolatry. But that was useless, since the Catholic Church, too, condemns the worship of Mary. Most important, I could find no good Protestant reason for the rejection of the Real Presence in the Eucharist when John 6 so clearly shows Jesus commanding His disciples to eat His Flesh, and historically all Christians believed this doctrine for the first 1500 years of Christianity. I finally knocked at the door at my local parish and began the process of entering the Church.

When I told my friends, they were mostly kind and accepting. Some tried to dissuade me from entering the Church. One friend, Donna, invited me to go to hear anti-Catholic apologist Bart Brewer speak about the Catholic Church at a large nondenominational church in a nearby town. I knew Brewer was an ex-priest and anti-Catholic, but I went anyway. The Easter Vigil was only months away. I wanted to let him take his best shot at me before I entered the Church. But as it turned out, his was just the same old attack on the Catholic Church without refuting the scriptural and historical evidence for her doctrines.

Brewer criticized and condemned the Catholic Church for relying on the "Bible plus the *Catechism,*" instead of relying on the Bible alone. But he himself was relying on the Bible plus Calvin's *Institutes.* Surprisingly, Donna saw through his double standard: he wasn't *sola Scriptura* either! She found him totally useless in helping her to "deprogram" me.

I embrace the "something else"

Eighteen months after my inquiry began, I entered the Holy Catholic Church at the Easter Vigil in 1999. Our four youngest children were received into the Catholic Church at Easter in 2000 with my husband's permission. My husband and three oldest children are still Protestant, but they are very

supportive — especially my husband. In fact, Mike is currently leading a Catholic/Protestant Bible study on the Gospel of John, with the stated purpose of teaching the biblical
basis for Catholic theology. At first, I thought he would
quickly follow me into the Church, but he has his own path to
follow on the journey of faith.

And — surprise! — Donna entered the Catholic Church
at Easter in 2002. She would have entered the previous year,
but she felt her husband needed more time to adjust to her
conversion.

I'm thankful to my Protestant teachers for the solid foundation they laid in me about the truths of Christianity and the
illusions of worldly passions, and for their encouragement to
study God's holy Word. It fed my soul for forty years. The irony
is that I studied the Bible so much that I uncovered many dis-
crepancies between some Protestant doctrines and Sacred
Scripture. This was the beginning of my loss of confidence in
Protestant Christianity.

But it wasn't until Catholic authors made me face the historical evidence that Christianity pre-existed the New Testament by four hundred years that I began to consider the
implications of this fact. That the Faith was alive, spreading
the gospel, establishing churches, instructing and baptizing
converts for so long (for reference, four hundred years ago was
about the time the Pilgrims came to America!) before the
New Testament was compiled, meant that the New Testament
couldn't be the touchstone of the Faith. The New Testament
was not the very first reservoir of Christian teaching.

Something else existed before it.

And that same "something else" kept the Faith alive and
gave birth to the New Testament. It was the oral teaching, the

deposit of the Faith of the Apostles, that was used to make the final decisions about which books would end up in the New Testament. No book was included in the canon of the New Testament that contradicted the Faith of the Apostles. And that is why, I discovered to my joy, nothing in Catholic doctrine contradicts anything in the Bible. The Bible, loved by Protestants as well as by Catholics, the inspired and inerrant Word of God, was written and published by the Catholic Church.

The icing on the cake of solid, scriptural Catholic doctrine was the beauty and poetry of Catholic worship. Its reverence in comparison with modern Evangelical praise services spoke to me of its ancient pedigree and authenticity. The Mass is ancient and Jewish — closer in form to Temple worship than to that of a Calvary Chapel. The ritual, the prayers, and the priestly robes are more Old Testament than those of my former Evangelical Free Church. And the incense and chants echo the heavenly worship found in the book of Revelation better than any Baptist service does.

In the end, a thousand tiny puzzle pieces of Bible verses, doctrines, prayers, history, martyrs, and liturgy came together to form for me a clear image of the one, holy, catholic, and apostolic Church.

"He who states his case first seems right, until the other comes and examines him."[46]

---

[46] Prov. 18:17.

An Anglican Priest
Discovers "More Christianity"

I left Bob Jones University and was ordained an Anglican priest so I could serve the ancient Church in England. Only later did I find that the ancient Church is the Catholic Church.

Dwight Longenecker

In the eighteenth century, my Mennonite ancestors left Switzerland for the new colony of Pennsylvania to find religious freedom. Seven generations later, they were still in Pennsylvania, but they had left the Mennonites, and I was brought up in a Bible church that was part of a loosely knit confederation of churches called the Independent Fundamental Churches of America.

The independent Bible church movement was an offshoot of a significant shift in postwar American Protestantism. Conservative Christians who were disenchanted with the liberal drift of the main Protestant denominations simply up and left and started their own churches.

The same independent movement saw the foundation of a fundamentalist college in the deep South by the Methodist evangelist Bob Jones. After World War II, my parents and aunts and uncles went to study there, and it was natural for my parents to send my brothers and sisters and me there in the 1970s.

From simplicity to splendor, via Bob Jones

The religion in our own home was simple, Bible-based, and balanced. I will always be thankful for the sincere and deep faith of my parents and will always regard with pride the great Christian heritage I was given. On both sides of the family, our people were committed Christians as far back as we could trace. At the heart of my family's faith — like that of our Mennonite and Plymouth Brethren forebears — there was a spirit of quiet simplicity and tolerance. We believed Catholics were in error, but we didn't nurture hatred toward them.

At Bob Jones University, the tone was different. There the Catholic Church was the "Whore of Babylon" and the Pope was the Antichrist. Besides the anti-Catholicism, there was a disagreeable whiff of the anti-Semitism and racism that marred Southern culture.

At Bob Jones University, I majored in interpretative speech, with a minor in English. I immersed myself in English literature and was greatly influenced by C. S. Lewis and his band of literary Christians, the Inklings. This drew me to the culture of England. A friend gave me a picture book called *The World of C. S. Lewis,* full of soft-focus photographs of Oxford quadrangles and people punting at Cambridge. There were black-and-white pictures of Lewis and his chums swilling dark beer in dim English pubs. The book was full of images of misty fields, quiet English rivers, the green and gold of the English countryside, roaring fires in Oxford common rooms, the heavenly glories of college chapels, and the homely glories of Anglican country churches. One look made me realize this was a world I wanted to enter.

Although the student body at Bob Jones University was predominantly independent Evangelical and Baptist, the school's own position was nondenominational: it welcomed believers from every (Protestant) denomination. The Episcopal Church was so liberal, however, that we probably wouldn't have been allowed to go there unless we were cradle Episcopalians. But as it happened, a member of the Bob Jones board was also a founding member of the deliciously named "Holy Trinity Anglican Orthodox Church," a little church that had broken away from the Episcopalians. I've always thought this wealthy man's "influence" was the reason we were allowed to attend.

The little breakaway church was founded by a "bishop" who drove a Lincoln Continental and had a taste for wine and for wealthy Episcopalian ladies. His orders were "valid, but irregular." He had been ordained twice: by a renegade Eastern Orthodox bishop and by a breakaway Catholic bishop. Despite its bizarre background, with more than a hint of corruption, this little Anglican Church connected us with a faith that felt more ancient than the local independent Bible Church. So along with some other Fundamentalists — some curious, others disenchanted — I went to the little stone church in the bad part of town and discovered there the glories of the *Book of Common Prayer,* lighting candles, and kneeling to pray. We learned to chant the Psalms, discovered Lent and Advent, and felt we were in touch with the religion of C. S. Lewis, the Inklings, and the great English writers.

Affirming all things in Oxford

While a student at Bob Jones, I visited England a couple of times, and feeling the call to the ministry, I wondered whether I might be ordained as an Anglican priest in England and perhaps look after one of the beautiful medieval churches in the English countryside. For any lover of C. S. Lewis, Oxford was a kind of Mecca; so when the opportunity came to study at Oxford, I jumped at the chance and went to England for good.

My three years at Oxford were a time of great growth and learning. Often it is the little bit of wisdom that makes the most impression, and I will never forget this quotation from the great Anglican socialist F. D. Maurice: "A man is most often right in what he affirms and wrong in what he denies."

After the negative attitudes of American fundamentalism and the cynical religious doubt that prevailed at Oxford, Maurice's statement was a breath of fresh air. I was sometimes tempted to feel guilty about leaving the religion of my family and upbringing, but Maurice's viewpoint assured me that the Anglican riches I was discovering were not a denial of my family faith, but an *addition* to it. I took Maurice's dictum as my motto, and whenever I came across something new, I asked whether I was denying or affirming. If I wasn't able to affirm the new doctrine or religious practice, I wouldn't deny it — I would simply let it be.

During my studies, this principle allowed me to explore the more Catholic aspects of Anglicanism. I discovered that T. S. Eliot was an "Anglo-Catholic"; that C. S. Lewis worshiped in his "high" college chapel and that his parish church in Headington was more Catholic than low-church. Dorothy Sayers and Charles Williams were also on the Catholic end of Anglicanism, and J. R. R. Tolkien was actually a Roman Catholic, as were Graham Greene and Evelyn Waugh. Through these writers I was increasingly drawn to the Catholic spiritual tradition in the Church of England. I did a special study of the history of the Anglo-Catholic Oxford Movement and attended a series of lectures on fourteenth-century English spiritual writers given by the English Dominican Simon Tugwell. When

I had the chance, I worshiped at Pusey House — one of the Anglo-Catholic student centers at Oxford — and found myself gravitating toward the high culture and high religion found in the college chapels and the Anglican cathedral at Christ Church. At Oxford it became clear to me that at the Lord's banquet, the Master was calling, "Friend, come up higher!"[47]

I continued to add to my Evangelical upbringing. C. S. Lewis had given me a love for "mere" Christianity;[48] I wanted "more" Christianity. Through Anglicanism I was able to explore the historical Faith while still holding to the Protestant basics that I considered non-negotiable. I also learned about social justice and zeal for serving the poor, and saw Anglicanism as a broad church that could include all these elements. While I was happy to be influenced by these other strands, like many Anglicans I also wanted my faith to be cross-fertilized by the good things of Roman Catholicism.

I discover the ancient Church

During my time at Oxford, an American Catholic friend named June suggested that I might like to visit a Benedictine monastery. I made my first visit and found myself drawn to the quiet life of prayer and study that the monks followed. After finishing my theological studies, I was ordained as a curate (assistant minister) in the Anglican Church. My ministry lasted four years and ended when I was in my late twenties.

When my curacy was finished, I had three months free and decided to hitchhike to Jerusalem. So with a backpack and a

---

[47] Cf. Luke 14:10.
[48] Cf. C. S. Lewis, *Mere Christianity*.

pair of sturdy shoes, I set out across France and Italy, staying in monasteries and convents along the route. I found my day's journey went best when I fit in with the monastic routine. I would begin each day with Mass and morning offices in one monastery, say my Anglican prayers while traveling, then arrive at the next monastery in time for Vespers,[49] the evening meal, and Night Prayer.

My pilgrimage to the Holy Land took me further into Christian history. Part of the appeal of being an Anglican was to leave the modern "do as you please" church of Protestant America and find deeper routes in the history and Faith of Europe. I had wanted to be part of the "ancient Church in England." Traveling through France, Italy, and Greece to Israel, I found myself immersed in a religion obviously older than Anglicanism. The Benedictine monasteries put me in touch with roots of Faith that were deeper and more concrete than I had imagined could exist. Although I realized my views were becoming more Catholic, I didn't fight it. I wanted to "be right in what I affirmed."

Anglo-Catholicism and fuzzy thinking

When I came back from the Holy Land, I went to be a chaplain at King's College in Cambridge. For two years, I shared in the most beautiful worship in one of the most sublime Christian buildings in the world. Although the Liturgy, music, and architecture were superb, religion at Cambridge was rotten with relativism and personal immorality. I knew I wasn't cut out for either the academic life or the cultured highlands of Anglicanism, so I began to look for a parish.

---

[49] Liturgical evening prayer.

An Anglican Priest Discovers "More Christianity"

My dream of being a country Anglican vicar came true when I went to be the parish priest of two beautiful old churches on the Isle of Wight, just off the southern coast of England. By this time, I had lived in England for ten years. I was in my early thirties and had moved quite far in my understanding of the Faith. Most of all, I had come to regard my ministry in a very Catholic way. I knew we Anglicans were separated from Rome, but I considered my ministry to be part of the whole Catholic Church. Despite our formal separation, I thought of Anglicanism as a branch of the Catholic Church, and I prayed for the time of our eventual reunion.

My pilgrimage thus far had been mostly intuitive. I simply adopted the Catholic practices that seemed suitable, and when it came time to consider certain doctrines, I made every effort to affirm and not deny. This mindset brought me almost unconsciously to the very doorstep of the Catholic Church. What I said to some friends who were considering conversion was true of me as well: I was more Catholic than I realized.

My thinking remained fuzzy for some time. Then, four years after I went to my parish, the Church of England voted to ordain women as priests. Although that decision had been brewing for a long time, I had put it to the side and not thought about it much. When the final vote came, my thinking cleared.

For me, women priests were not the problem; rather, it was what the General Synod's decision-making process revealed about the true nature of the Church of England. For if the Anglican Church were truly a part of the Catholic Church, she did not have the authority to ordain women as priests; but if the Anglican Church were Protestant, then, like all Protestant groups, she could do whatever she wanted.

When the General Synod made the decision, I was put in a quandary. Everything within me said that a church that claimed to be Catholic could not make this decision on her own. Yet I hated to take a negative position about anything. According to my motto that a person is "right in what he affirms and wrong in what he denies," I was wrong to deny women priests.

The other side of affirmation

Then a Catholic friend gently pointed out that greater affirmations often include smaller denials. In other words, you can't have everything. Choices need to be made. Denying women priests was merely the negative side of affirming something greater — apostolic succession of Church authority. Affirming Catholicism required denial of those things contrary to Catholicism.

Once I began to look again at the different churches and the claims of the Catholic Church, I saw how very strange it was to have so many different Christian denominations. Jesus commanded that there be "one flock and one Shepherd,"[50] but we quite happily made thousands of flocks with thousands of shepherds! Worse, the different Protestant denominations were identified, not by what they affirmed, but by what they denied. So, for example, the Baptists were known not so much for a mode of baptism, but by their denial of infant Baptism. The Anglicans were known not so much for their allegiance to a corrupt and depraved King Henry VIII, but by their denial of the papacy. And what united all the Protestants, and made them bedfellows with all sorts of atheists and non-Christians, was their shared denial of the claims of the Catholic Church.

[50] Cf. John 10:16.

"Then all of us ought to be Catholics"

If I was wrong in what I denied, could it be that, as a Protestant, I was wrong in my denial of the claims of the Catholic Church?

I began to study the writings of the early Church Fathers and got a copy of the *Catechism of the Catholic Church*. In our parish Bible study, I took our people through a study of the New Testament Church. We considered the role Jesus gave the Apostles. We considered what St. Paul had to say about the Church. We considered the New Testament's clear teaching that Church unity must be maintained at all costs.[51] We confronted the verses that taught that the Church was built on the foundation of the Apostles and that God made manifest His wisdom through the Church[52] — the Church that is the "pillar and foundation of truth."[53] I was stunned when one woman in the Bible study said, "If what you are saying is right, Vicar, all of us ought to become Roman Catholics!" She had drawn the very conclusion from which I was trying to run away.

When I began to express my own increasing convictions about the claims of the Catholic Church, people were shocked and upset. Some had listened closely to my preaching and had seen the crisis coming. Others were angry and accusatory. I was being disloyal to my own Church, or even worse, I was calling their Christian life into question. Still others were confused and frustrated. Their feelings were summed up by a good Methodist woman who came to our church with her

---

[51] Eph. 4:3-6; 1 Cor. 1:10-13.
[52] Eph. 3:10.
[53] Cf. 1 Tim. 3:15.

Anglican husband: "Surely the only thing that matters is how much we love Jesus!"

Her statement is difficult to answer, not because there is no answer, but because there are too many answers. In a letter to an inquirer, Cardinal Newman said, "Catholicism is a matter; it cannot be taken in a teacup." He meant that Catholicism was so vast, and the reasons for conversion so overwhelming and complex, that it is impossible to sum up the whole thing in a neat and pithy formula.

The Jesus in the mirror

In one sense, the good Methodist woman was right. It could be said that the only thing that matters *is* how much we love Jesus. Hers is the right answer, but it is also the right question: How much do we love Jesus, and how can we be sure that we love Jesus and not just our idea of Jesus?

I had seen many Jesuses among different Christians, and each was strangely like that particular Christian. Charismatics saw a Spirit-filled prophet of God. People concerned with justice and peace saw a radical revolutionary who spoke for the poor. Intellectuals saw a Jesus who was cleverer than anybody else and suffered for it. Tasteful Christians at Cambridge saw a Jesus who was a kind of persecuted agnostic poet. Snobs saw a lofty Jesus who was head and shoulders above everyone else, and working-class people saw Jesus the humble carpenter.

I began to see that my Jesus was also a reflection of myself. I'm inclined to be intellectual, contemplative, and intuitive. I followed a Jesus who pondered problems, went out to the wilderness to pray, and found crowds of people difficult. My Jesus walked a lonely path to a distant Cross because that's how I was walking through life myself.

Searching for the universal Christ

But to follow Christ should mean to lose yourself, not to worship yourself. I wanted an objective Jesus — one who was not my own reflection. I wanted a Christ who was cosmic, not a Christ who was comfy. Where was this Jesus to be found? In the Incarnation. In His body.

Where was His Body to be found? The Scriptures were clear: the Body of Christ was the Church. St. Paul was inspired to use this image for the Church.

I had been taught that the Church was the Body of Christ in a symbolic way, that all of us in a particular congregation should work together like members of a body. But the emphasis in that teaching was on only half of the image: it stressed *body* — not *Christ*. When I put the two together and saw the Church as the Body of Christ, a window opened.

As an Evangelical, I was taught that the different churches were man-made organizations that were useful, but essentially unnecessary. Now I saw the Church as the Mystical Body of Christ — a living, dynamic organism empowered by the Holy Spirit to continue the work of the risen Lord in the world.

The Church was suddenly a sacrament of Christ. In my brothers and sisters, I could find Jesus. In my service to the Church, I could find Jesus. In our worship, I could find Jesus. In obedience to the teaching of the Church, I could find Jesus. By immersing myself in the Church, I immersed myself in Jesus and transcended the limitations of my personal walk with the Lord.

But if my Church was only a gathering of people like me, and if Jesus was only a reflection of us, then we were serving ourselves, not Him.

139

I began to feel that my experience of Christ within the Anglican Church was simply a larger version of the individualistic Christ I had experienced within Evangelicalism. If the Evangelical Christian was inclined to find a "Jesus" who was rather like himself, the same problem could arise on a denominational level. I began to see that Anglicans worshiped a very Anglican Jesus. He was a refined, softly spoken gentleman. He was tolerant, tasteful, and forgiving. He was persecuted by barbaric, bigoted religious people. There was much that was good and true in this Anglican portrait of Jesus, but there was also a fair bit missing. If individual Christians made Jesus in their own image, so did the various denominations.

The problem with a Jesus who is only personal is that He becomes private property. There are only two ways around this problem. One is the Anglican way, in which every opinion is tolerated and encouraged. By allowing every personal Jesus — even heretical ones — the Anglican hopes to obtain a comprehensive Jesus. This is the way of latitudinarianism or indifferentism.

The other option is to break away into a little Christian group in which everyone shares the same vision of Jesus. That vision becomes the only one. This second way is known as sectarianism.

With the first option, every type of personal Christ is tolerated; with the second, only one. But surely both ways had an element of truth? All the different personal Jesuses reflected a dimension of Jesus Christ, but there had to be one that was the fullest, most complete experience of Christ. Somewhere there had to be a Church that embraced all the varied portraits of Jesus while still holding up an objective Christ who transcended and completed all the partial portraits.

The marks of true authority

If Jesus' promise always to be with us was true, and if the Church was the Mystical Body of Christ, there had to be a Church that presented an objective Christ to the world in a personal way.

How could any one denomination hope to present such a cosmic view of Christ, since they were all founded by particular men at particular points in time for certain historical reasons? For any church to present a Christ big enough to conquer our individual portraits of Jesus, it would have to speak with a special authority.

To offer a universal Christ in a personal way, the Church would have to speak with an authority that was bigger than any one individual or denominational group. To offer a universal Christ, that authority would have certain traits. I began to draw up a list to outline what those traits should be.

First, such an authority would need to be *historical*. To give me a Jesus that was bigger than me, this church's teaching and experience had to be rooted in history. Through her roots in history, I could share in a Christian experience that transcended my own personal feelings and cultural background.

Second, this authority must be *objective*. It couldn't be subject to my personal whim or the whims of my local pastor or of any local prophet or teacher. It would have to reach beyond the individual benefits of its leaders or members. To prove its objectivity, this authority had to be spread out over a large number of people over a long period, while remaining consistent in its themes and purpose.

Third, this authority should be *universal*. It couldn't be the voice of just one person, one nationality, one theological faction, or one pressure group. This authority had to transcend geographical, cultural, and intellectual boundaries. Not only did it have to be universal geographically; it had to transcend time as well. It had to be universal down through time, connecting authentically with every age.

Fourth, it must also be *particular*. The authority must be specified in a particular place and through a particular person. It cannot be just a vague body of teaching or "consensus of the faithful." To speak to me personally, it has to speak with a clear, particular, and authentic voice. It also has to be able to apply the universal truths of the gospel to particular problems with confidence.

Fifth, this authority should be *intellectually satisfying*. Although it must be simple enough for every person to understand and obey, it must also be challenging enough for the world's greatest philosophers. As St. Jerome[54] said of Scripture, "It must be shallow enough for a lamb to wade and deep enough for an elephant to swim." This authority must be intellectually coherent within itself and able to engage other intellectual religions and philosophical systems. Furthermore, if it is intellectually satisfying, it must offer a world view that is complete without being completely closed. In other words, within it there must be answers as well as questions that still remain.

Sixth, this authority must be *scriptural*. Since Scripture is a primary witness to revelation, this authority needs to be rooted in Scripture and founded on Scripture. If it is scriptural, it will look to Scripture continually as a source of inspiration and guidance. Although this authority will flow from Scripture, it

---

[54] St. Jerome (c. 342-420), Doctor who translated the Bible into Latin.

will also confirm Scripture and offer the right interpretation of Scripture with confidence — never contradicting Scripture, but always working to illuminate it further.

I concluded that if an authority could be shown to fulfill all six of these traits, then that authority is not ephemeral and merely human, but is of divine origin. If such an authority could be found, it could give my personal experience of Jesus Christ the universal depth and breadth that lifts me out of the worship of Jesus in my own image, which is essentially the worship of myself.

The only place such an authority even claims to exist is in the Catholic Church.

I concluded that my Faith had to be Catholic if it was to be universal, but I still felt that I could be a good Catholic while remaining an Anglican. (According to my Evangelical viewpoint, since denominations didn't matter, I could subscribe to Catholic views while remaining in another denomination.)

From Anglo-Catholic to fully Catholic

But one thing still ate away at me. How could I claim to be Catholic while I was rejecting one of the basic characteristics of Catholicism — full communion with the head of the family of the Catholic Church, the Bishop of Rome?

I was denying the authority of the Pope, and F. D. Maurice's dictum now echoed in me as a condemnation, not as a force for liberation. Was I wrong in my denial? Could I claim to be Catholic while rejecting the rock on which the Catholic Church was built?

I then came across Cardinal Newman's famous *Essay on the Development of Christian Doctrine*. In a dense but clear passage he says:

If Christianity is both social and dogmatic, and intended for all ages, it must, humanly speaking, have an infallible expounder, else you will secure unity of form at the loss of unity of doctrine, or unity of doctrine at the loss of unity of form; you will have to choose between a comprehension of opinions and a resolution into parties; between latitudinarian and sectarian error. . . . You must accept the whole or reject the whole. . . . [I]t is trifling to receive all but something which is as integral as any other portion. Thus it would be trifling indeed to accept everything Catholic except the head of the Body of Christ on earth.

In other words, if I wanted the universal Jesus that Catholicism offered, I had to embrace Catholicism too. But to have Catholicism, I couldn't pick and choose. How could I have fullness of the Faith when I was still the one choosing what is "full" and what isn't? To accept the Body of Christ in its fullness, I had to accept it all. That's what *fullness* implies: If you want to be Catholic, you have to accept the ministry of the Bishop of Rome.

By now I was married, and we had two young children. I had been in the parish for seven years. The Isle of Wight was a beautiful place to live and bring up a family. Not wanting to give up my ministry and my beautiful home, churches, and congregations, I decided to "accept the Pope" but remain in the Anglican Church.

Yet soon it became clear that I could not accept the Pope without submitting to his teaching, and that a vital part of his teaching was that to enjoy the fullness of the Faith, I had to be in full communion with the Faith.

St. Paul's words haunted me: "Because there is one bread, we who are many are one body, for we all partake of the one bread."[55] Eventually I saw that the only way for my personal vision of Jesus to be enlarged to a universal experience of the risen Lord was for me to be received into full communion and personal union with His Body on earth — the universal Church.

I join the ancient Church in England

The next few months were a terrible time of indecision. Together, my wife, Alison, and I contemplated the future. We had planned on a settled and happy life of ministry in the Anglican Church. I hadn't trained for any other career, and if we left the Anglican Church, there seemed nothing but an uncertain future. Could we possibly leave everything and step out into the unknown? Surely it was possible to stay in the Anglican Church a bit longer.

Then one Sunday evening I went to Quarr Abbey — a local Catholic Benedictine abbey — for Vespers and Benediction. This modern abbey is built just a few hundred yards from the ruins of a medieval abbey. As the monks chanted, I agonized over the decision to leave the Church of England.

"Why this call to become a Catholic?" I cried out to the Lord. "I only wanted to serve You in the ancient Church in England!"

As the incense wafted heavenward and Christ's Body was lifted for us to adore, the still, small voice replied, "But *this* is the ancient Church in England."

Then the struggles ended. My mind was made up.

[55] 1 Cor. 10:17.

In the autumn of 1994, my wife and I began our course of instruction to be received into the Church.

When I became an Anglican, I felt my Bible-Christian background was being completed, not denied. As we prepared to be received into the Catholic Church, I realized that the same was true as we became Catholics. I could still affirm everything my non-Catholic friends and family affirmed; I just could no longer deny what they denied.

F. D. Maurice's little snippet of wisdom had brought me across the Tiber, and in becoming a Catholic, I was affirming all of Christ's truth without a shred of denial. Furthermore, I felt that I had stepped into a Church as vast, ancient, and full of fascinating detail as one of the medieval cathedrals. The vistas were huge, and there always seemed to be more and more and more things to affirm. Indeed, joyful affirmation — not sour denial — was one of the basic rules of this new country.

Our reception took place in a quiet service one February evening in the crypt of Quarr Abbey church. That night all was harvest. As the monks sang and we were finally received into full communion, the simple faith of my Mennonite forebears, the Bible Christians' love of the Scriptures, and the ancient beauties of Anglicanism were gathered together and fulfilled in a new and dynamic way in Christ's one, holy, catholic, and apostolic Church.

"More Catholic Than the Pope" No More

The beauty of the Tridentine Latin Mass drew me into a group of ultratraditional Catholic separatists. From there the popes called me back into full communion with them.

Pete Vere, JCL

Who would want to read a story about someone who left the Catholic Church, joined the Lefebvre schism, then came back? Stories like mine are few and far between, unlike those of the great number of Protestants who annually convert to Catholicism. Yet my story really isn't so different: Martin Luther and Marcel Lefebvre shared more than their initials and the sacrament of Holy Orders — they shared a common spirit of private interpretation and private judgment.

In a futile attempt to recover what he perceived as an earlier and purer form of Christianity, each separated himself from full communion with the Church founded by Christ. In so doing, Luther and Lefebvre both rebelled against the Church's living Magisterium. They asserted their own private interpretation — of Scripture in the one case and Tradition in the other — over the authoritative interpretation of the Roman Pontiff, who, as St. Peter's successor, is entrusted with the task of safeguarding both Scripture and Tradition. Each man's actions led to movements that continue to divide into ever smaller sects, since with private interpretation every individual enjoys his own little papacy. This is in spite of the fact the first followers of both movements steadfastly believed that they were still Catholic.

During my time as a Lefebvrite schismatic, I believed it too.

Searching for spiritual power

At the age of sixteen, I was a self-styled Satanist. I had been raised a Catholic, but felt anger toward the Church. Yet my father and my teachers had fostered in me a deep devotion to the Blessed Mother, and I made a regular practice of praying the Rosary. I knew in my heart that Mary had helped me through many childhood problems, so even though I hated the Church, I couldn't bring myself to abandon the Blessed Mother. I engaged in minor satanic practices while wearing a brown scapular!

This changed suddenly when I switched schools and met a new friend, Dave, who was born and raised Pentecostal. I went with him one day to his church, where I was immediately fascinated by the lively music. Having grown up in the Catholic Church during the confusions after the Second Vatican Council, I had found Sunday Mass boring and banal. Pentecostalism was Christianity as I had never encountered: alive, exciting, and dynamic. It offered me a sense of spiritual power, something I had previously sought through Satanism. Only in Pentecostalism did I feel the power of Christ's gospel and the Holy Spirit's touch.

I joined the Pentecostal church and stayed in it for about three years. There I came to love the Bible, the power of the Holy Spirit, and the truth of the Christian message. Yet as I neared my nineteenth birthday, I started looking elsewhere.

Although many doctrinal issues influenced my decision to leave the Pentecostal church, at the heart of my exodus was a deep loneliness. As a Christian teenager, I needed peer support from other teens. But most of my Pentecostal friendships were transitory: every week new faces came into our church, accepted Jesus as their Lord and Savior, and got saved; but most soon lost their zeal for the gospel, fell away, and returned to their former worldly ways. In the three years after I dedicated my life to Christ in the Pentecostal church, I saw hundreds of other teenagers come and go, and only a few remain.

This depressed me and hardened my heart. Cynical remnants of my involvement with Satanism returned. My condition worsened when one of our pastors, also saddened by the attrition, announced from the pulpit that he was resigning to join a Calvinist church. He then preached about a vengeful God who predestined most souls to Hell and merely a handful to Heaven. This unmerciful God repulsed me, and thus our Lord opened my heart to seeking Him elsewhere.

Following Tradition right out of the Church

Then, through my father, I met Irene, an elderly woman prone to illness who was respected within our local community as a staunch Roman Catholic. She introduced me to St. Faustina's Chaplet of Divine Mercy,[56] a devotion I took to almost immediately. This Catholic devotion didn't bother me as a Protestant since there was no mention in it of Mary or the saints. Faustina's merciful God contrasted with the vengeful

---

[56] A series of short prayers invoking God's mercy, prayed using rosary beads. The chaplet is part of the Divine Mercy devotion begun by St. Faustina Kowalska (1905-1938), a Sister of Our Lady of Mercy, after she saw a vision in 1931.

God proposed by my former pastor. I started working through some doctrinal issues, and soon I knew God was calling me back to the Church in which I had been born and raised.

Yet Irene was not a Catholic like those I remembered from church during my youth. Rather, she was a "Traditional" Catholic. She followed a French archbishop who had run into problems with the Vatican after the Second Vatican Council: Marcel Lefebvre.

Archbishop Lefebvre had spent most of his ecclesiastical career as a missionary to Africa. After retiring in Rome during the late '60s, he grew concerned about many of the abuses arising in the Church at that time, particularly in the areas of doctrine and Liturgy. The archbishop blamed Vatican II for spreading these abuses, and after being contacted by priests, seminarians, and faithful laymen with similar concerns, he came out of retirement and founded the Society of St. Pius X (SSPX), named after the pope who had written the encyclical *Pascendi*, which condemned the modernist heresy.[57]

The rallying point for Archbishop Lefebrve and his followers is the old Liturgy offered in Latin. Many commonly refer to this Liturgy as the Traditional or Tridentine Mass, since Pope St. Pius V codified it soon after the Council of Trent in his 1570 papal bull *Quo Primum Tempore*. The SSPX embraces the Tridentine Mass, said in Latin with the priest's back to the people, and rejects the "new" Liturgy adopted by the Church in 1969 and offered throughout the world in the vernacular, as well as in Latin. The SSPX's rejection of the Liturgy, and

---

[57] A complex heresy, difficult to define simply, but marked generally by rejection of the supernatural, weakening of Church authority, and religious indifferentism.

violations of Church law by Archbishop Lefebvre and others, soon placed the society in a state of schism — willful separation from the corporate unity of the Church.

In codifying the Tridentine Liturgy in *Quo Primum Tempore*, St. Pius V promulgated the Tridentine Mass "in perpetuity," meaning for all time. On this basis, the SSPX claims that every priest has the right to use the old Tridentine Roman Missal and that this right cannot be taken away from him.[58] *Quo Primum Tempore* was the first argument from an SSPX apologist I encountered, and the one that led me into schism with them.

Necessary disobedience?

Despite her physical illness, Irene taught me much of this and loaned me numerous books on the saints, the Rosary, the

[58] During my canonical studies, I discovered that the *Quo Primum Tempore* argument failed to take into account the canonical Tradition of the Church. This argument confused the difference between the Church's doctrine and her discipline. A dogma is a doctrine the Church declares with certitude to be infallible. It binds the entire Church. A discipline of the Faith, on the other hand, is a practice originating from the Church as a means of safeguarding the good order of the Church. It need not bind the entire Church and is subject to change, depending upon the present needs of the Church. Within the text of *Quo Primum Tempore*, St. Pius V promulgates a clause exempting the use of his missal for all priests and bishops who were using liturgical missals older than two hundred years. Therefore, *Quo Primum Tempore* never applied to every Catholic priest. It must therefore be disciplinary, rather than dogmatic, in nature. As mere discipline, it is subject to change or revocation by a future Roman Pontiff, such as Pope Paul VI, since, in accordance with canonical Tradition, "equals have no power over one another."

Eucharist, the Tridentine Liturgy, and other topics relating to the SSPX schism. She introduced me to the local SSPX community, which made due with a makeshift altar in the basement of a union hall when the SSPX priest visited twice a month. The beauty and the solemnity of the Latin Tridentine Liturgy impressed me, and I noticed the reverence and faith of the people in attendance. Nevertheless, I wondered why they were forced to attend Mass in a basement when local parishes abounded.

When I raised this question with the SSPX priest, he explained that we weren't able to use any local parish because Rome had attempted to excommunicate members of the SSPX in 1988 when the archbishop consecrated four bishops without permission from the Holy Father. This troubled me, because I knew that Catholics were bound to obey the Pope. However, the priest claimed that faith was greater than obedience and that, in order to obey God, we must sometimes disobey Church authorities.

This answer satisfied me for a time, but then the question of Archbishop Lefebvre's excommunication began to bother me. After all, was Pope John Paul II not the head of the Church, and had he not publicly excommunicated Archbishop Lefebvre? On his next visit to our town, the SSPX chaplain assured me the archbishop's excommunication was invalid according to Canon Law: the Church had never truly excommunicated the archbishop or members of the SSPX. The priest maintained that one can ignore Canon Law when a "state of necessity" exists in the Church, and because so many Catholics lost their faith after the Second Vatican Council, a state of necessity obviously existed. I accepted the priest's explanation.

Who can you trust to interpret Tradition?

Then I began to wonder what in fact a state of necessity was, since the SSPX constantly appealed to it in order to justify disobedience to the Holy Father. When I approached our SSPX chaplain a second time with this question, he quoted the theories of a few canonists from before the Second Vatican Council, but never provided me with the Church's actual definition of this term. He avoided answering the question directly, something that alarmed me since this was the justification for our existence. Now every time I walked down the aisle of our local SSPX chapel to receive Holy Communion, the question haunted me: Was I in schism?

And how could I even be sure I was following true Catholic Tradition? I knew there were groups that offered the same Tridentine Liturgy as the SSPX, but with full permission of the Pope and the local bishop. I knew various sedevacantist[59] groups also offered the Latin Tridentine Mass, but believed John Paul II to be an anti-pope. These groups all claimed to follow Catholic Tradition, but they disagreed with one another about the present Pope, the authenticity of the Second Vatican Council, and the validity of the Mass offered in the English language. Who was right?

In response to my doubts, my SSPX spiritual director explained to me what the SSPX calls "doctrine-sifting." Basically, he accused all the other groups of either being too far to the left or too far to the right, while claiming the SSPX followed a middle road that acknowledged the errors of the modern popes without denying that these men truly held the papal

---

[59] Sedevacantistism (from the Latin for "empty chair") is the belief that there currently exists no validly elected Pope.

office. What the SSPX does, I was told, is to sift the statements originating from Rome in order to separate authentic Catholic teaching from modern error.

I was appalled. Had I not previously renounced Protestant fundamentalism, which, through private Scripture interpretation, made every man his own sect? Yet my SSPX spiritual director now offered me a similar notion of private interpretation, substituting Denzinger's *Enchiridion Symbolorum*[60] for the Bible. Rigid private interpretation of previous papal texts was, in fact, a major cause of division among Traditional Catholics — division from the Church in some cases and from each other in almost every case.

Christ and His Vicar personify Tradition

By Divine Providence, one day my father interrupted my inner theological struggle and asked me to clean out the basement. There I found a forgotten box full of old papal encyclicals from my father's college days. At the bottom lay Pope Pius XII's *Mystici Corporis*. Curious, I opened it up to the following passage:

> But we must not think that [Jesus Christ] rules only in a hidden or extraordinary manner. On the contrary, our Redeemer also governs His Mystical Body in a visible and normal way through His Vicar on earth. . . . Since He was all wise, He could not leave the body of the Church he had founded as a human society without a visible head. . . . That Christ and His Vicar constitute only one Head is the solemn teaching of Our

---

[60] A nineteenth-century compendium of Catholic doctrine.

predecessor of immortal memory Boniface VIII in the Apostolic Letter *Unam Sanctam;* and his successors have never ceased to repeat the same.

"Of course," I thought to myself, "the Roman Pontiff and Jesus Christ form but one head of the Catholic Church." This means they speak with one voice. The word *tradition*, I recalled from various homilies I had heard in SSPX chapels, comes from the Latin verb *tradere*, "to hand down." I realized there must be a source from which Tradition was first handed down: that source is Jesus Christ.

Tradition, therefore, is a Person.

He is the Second Person of the Holy Trinity, who was incarnated in the womb of an immaculately conceived virgin. As Christ and His Vicar constitute but one Head of the Church, so the voice of Tradition must speak through St. Peter and his lawful successors in the Roman primacy. How could I embrace the voice of Catholic Tradition while rejecting the Rock, the person who on earth embodies that Tradition?

My confidence in the SSPX was shaken. Still, I knew my spiritual director was a young priest and that he sometimes misunderstood the SSPX's positions. So I signed up for an Ignatian retreat[61] offered by the society, hoping to find answers there. I was twenty-one years old and had been involved with the Lefebvre schism for three years.

A reform or a revolt?

On the first morning of the retreat, our SSPX retreat master introduced us to the Ignatian principle of charitable

---

[61] A retreat developed by St. Ignatius of Loyola (1491-1556), founder of the Jesuit Order.

interpretation. In a nutshell, this principle binds us as Catholics always to attach the most charitable interpretation to another man's words. This principle applies in particular, the retreat master explained, to instruction and direction given by our lawful ecclesiastical superiors.

Then, to my astonishment, he began criticizing perceived ambiguities of the Second Vatican Council, particularly *Dignitatis Humanae*, the council's Declaration on Religious Freedom. He related how, as the SSPX commonly claims, Archbishop Lefebvre refused to sign that document.

I was stunned. For the first time since I had joined ranks with the SSPX, issues stewing inside me burst forth.

If, as this priest maintained, the Ignatian principle of charitable interpretation applies most especially to our lawful ecclesiastical superiors, how could he openly criticize the council fathers and Pope John Paul II about alleged ambiguities? Was this priest not obliged to interpret such ambiguities as charitably as possible? Did he not believe John Paul II, as St. Peter's successor, to be the SSPX's legitimate ecclesiastical superior? For that matter, if the Ignatian principle of charitable interpretation applied in every situation, why was my bookcase full of SSPX books that consistently cast negative light upon every papal act and document after Vatican II?

I now admitted to myself what I already knew within my conscience to be true: I was in schism from Rome and must reconcile with the Church. But I still wasn't completely convinced that I ought to abandon the SSPX. I spoke to a friend at the retreat, an SSPX priest who struggled with some of the same questions. He urged me not to abandon the SSPX, claiming that the society was *headed* toward schism, but not there yet, and that it could still be reformed from inside.

I pondered his words. The thought of other Lefebvrite souls seeking to restore communion with Rome weighed on my conscience. Moreover, I wondered, could I abandon the many friends and acquaintances I knew through the SSPX? And what about other friends I had introduced to the SSPX? Could I leave them in a schism to which I had led them?

I needed to get away and think. By Divine Providence, a seminarian friend of mine was on retreat at a nearby Benedictine monastery. Knowing that at a monastery I could rest for a week and think things over, I ignored my spiritual director's pleas and left the SSPX retreat a day early.

A surprising signature

My friend greeted me at the monastery with a surprised look on his face and invited me to attend Vespers with him. I declined because the monks followed the modern Liturgy of Pope Paul VI, which I still viewed with suspicion. So my friend left me a copy of the March 1994 issue of *Fidelity* magazine, pointing out an article by Fr. Brian Harrison, "Marcel Lefebvre: Signatory to *Dignitatis Humanae.*" For the second time in less than a week, God answered my prayers by shattering my false conceptions of the SSPX. The article included a photographic reproduction of Archbishop Lefebvre's signature on *Dignitatis Humanae*. While the SSPX had led me to believe Lefebvre refused to sign this Vatican II document, this piece of evidence was undeniable. Archbishop Lefebvre clearly signed the document.

Why had the SSPX misled me?

As I pondered this, my friend returned from Vespers, and we spent the next hour debating the merits of the Second Vatican Council. I accused Pope Paul VI of watering down the

Church's theology of the Eucharist through his liturgical reform. My friend just smiled and passed me a little booklet.

"Here," he said, "read this." Glancing at the cover, I saw
that it was Pope Paul VI's 1965 papal encyclical *Mysterium
Fidei*. I returned to my cell and began reading it.

Vatican II sought to safeguard eucharistic teaching

At that time, I believed, like many Lefebvrites, that Paul
VI had intended to diminish, weaken, or break from the
Church's traditional eucharistic theology. Imagine my surprise, then, when I read this encyclical and discovered that
the Pope of the Council, the Pope of the "new Mass," was determined to uphold the Church's traditional teaching concerning the Most Holy Sacrament of the Eucharist, as well as
to condemn false teachings that had begun to surface within
the Church. *Mysterium Fidei* provided the key to help me
unlock the authentic interpretation of the Second Vatican
Council in light of the Church's sacred Tradition.

In the opening paragraph of *Mysterium Fidei*, Pope Paul VI
introduces the Catholic faithful to the mind of the council
fathers:

> The Catholic Church has always devoutly guarded
> as a most precious treasure the mystery of Faith, that is,
> the ineffable gift of the Eucharist which she received
> from Christ her Spouse as a pledge of His immense love,
> and during the Second Vatican Council in a new and
> solemn demonstration she professed her faith and ven-
> eration for this mystery. When dealing with the restora-
> tion of the sacred Liturgy, the Fathers of the council, by

reason of their pastoral concern for the whole Church, considered it of the highest importance to exhort the faithful to participate actively with sound faith and with the utmost devotion in the celebration of this Most Holy Mystery, to offer it with the priest to God as a sacrifice for their own salvation and for that of the whole world, and to find in it spiritual nourishment.

In other words, the Second Vatican Council sought not to deny the Holy Mystery of the Mass, but to safeguard its central role in the sanctification of Christ's faithful. Pope Paul VI strongly reaffirms the sacrificial aspect of the Mass in which our Lord's Real Presence is offered up to God the Father for the salvation of the individual and of the whole world. Although I had objected to the liturgical reform as an attempt to "Protestantize" the Church, Paul VI reassured me in *Mysterium Fidei* that the reform's true purpose was to address a pastoral concern of the council fathers, who felt the faithful had lost touch with the Holy Sacrifice of the Mass. As Pope Paul VI firmly stated, the fathers sought a more active lay participation in the eucharistic Liturgy in order to strengthen the Catholic faithful in the Church's traditional eucharistic doctrine and piety.

Thus, *Mysterium Fidei* opened my eyes, showing me that the Church's eucharistic Tradition had a clear voice in the teachings of Pope Paul VI and the Second Vatican Council.

Could Paul VI do any better than Jesus?

Another realization soon hit me as I sat reading. When many of Jesus' disciples begin abandoning Him after His teaching on the Eucharist in John 6, it is St. Peter who upholds our

Lord's teachings as "the words of eternal life."[62] Against the unbelief of the world, St. Peter responds with the faith made possible by grace. Could any less be expected of Paul VI, St. Peter's successor, when the same eucharistic doubts arose around the time of the Second Vatican Council?

I had wanted to believe Paul VI helped *cause* those doubts by promulgating his liturgical reform, yet how successful was St. Peter in bringing back those who abandoned Christ in the above Gospel account? Like his predecessor St. Peter, in the face of mass apostasy Pope Paul VI could only *uphold* the teachings of Christ and leave the rest to our Lord's capacity to work His grace in the hardened hearts of men.

That night I lay awake in bed, pondering how in *Mysterium Fidei* Paul VI made St. Peter's profession of faith in Jesus Christ his own and upheld a sacred mystery we cannot fully comprehend. Paul VI responded to the impending crisis in faith about the Holy Eucharist by professing the words of Jesus Christ. If people now abandoned the Church's traditional eucharistic teachings, it was not because Pope Paul VI had failed to proclaim the truth in an age of apostasy.

Up until this point, I had adhered to the SSPX because I believed it to be a restoration movement within the Church. Now I realized I could not save the Church; rather it is the Church that saves me. I began investigating the *Ecclesia Dei* movement,[63] through which Pope John Paul II allowed those

---

[62] John 6:68.

[63] *Ecclesia Dei adflicta* is the document Pope John Paul II promulgated in response to Archbishop Lefebvre's 1988 schism. After declaring the excommunication against Archbishop Lefebvre and his followers for consecrating bishops without the Holy Father's permission, Pope John Paul II asked the

who felt attached to the Tridentine Liturgy to remain in or to return to full communion with Rome. There I could work to preserve the old Latin Liturgy *within* the Church, rather than attempt a reform within a movement that had sadly severed communion with the Church.

Irene and I leave the SSPX

By now everyone knew that Irene's death was near. I stopped by the hospital and asked her to pray the Rosary with me, but she lacked the strength. We sat there for a moment as she fought the temptation to sleep. Suddenly, her eyes lit up with a fresh spark of life.

"Pete," she said, "God has given me a little strength. Let's pray the Divine Mercy chaplet." Instinctively knowing this would be our last prayer together this side of Heaven, we recited the chaplet amid tears. A warm sense of trust in Christ's Mystical Body overcame me, not unlike the glow that came across Irene's face. Christ was looking after His Church, just as He promised in the Gospels, and He would look after both Irene and me.

Afterward, I shared with her my fears and concerns about the SSPX. I told her that, as a Catholic, I could no longer, in good conscience, adhere to the SSPX or pretend their schism did not exist. I told her I must return to full communion with the Church.

"Peter," Irene replied softly, "you know where Christ is calling you. You know where to find Tradition. Just do what you have to do."

bishops of the world to permit, within their respective dioceses, a wider celebration of the sacraments according to the Latin Tridentine Liturgy.

About a month later, I attended my last Lefebvrite Liturgy — a solemn requiem Mass for the repose of Irene's soul. Our journeys out of the SSPX ended together.

I struggle to accept full communion with the post-conciliar Church

Through God's grace, I spent the next three years pursuing a licentiate degree in Canon Law from St. Paul University in Ottawa, Canada. I wrestled with the major arguments put forward by followers of Archbishop Lefebvre, arguments that had once drawn me into their schism and still lay unresolved in my mind, despite my having reconciled with the Church.[64]

Although I was no longer with the SSPX, during these years I continued to doubt the authenticity of the Second Vatican Council, as well as the validity of the sacraments offered according to the revised Liturgy of Pope Paul VI. I still had what many would call a remnant mentality: I believed that only those who exclusively attended the Tridentine Liturgy were fully Catholic. Thus, as a member of the *Ecclesia Dei* movement, I believed myself part of a Catholic remnant.

---

[64] The most difficult canonical argument I encountered was the SSPX's state-of-necessity argument based on canons 1323:4° and 1324 §1:5°. But God blessed me with the opportunity to have many private discussions with a highly respected canonist, who took an active interest in helping me resolve this and many other canonical controversies surrounding Archbishop Lefebvre's schism. He showed me that the state-of-necessity canons apply only in certain circumstances unforeseen by the Church. He pointed out that the Holy See foresaw the circumstances in which Archbishop Lefebvre found himself and that Archbishop Lefebvre simply refused to yield to the Holy See's analysis of the situation prior to consecrating bishops without Rome's approval.

I often argued this point with my best friend, Eric, an accountant and middle-age bachelor I had met through the Knights of Columbus. Eric firmly believed in the infallibility of the Petrine Office and the indefectibility of the Catholic Church, and he had a deep devotion to the Blessed Mother and the Holy Eucharist. As our new Grand Knight, Eric often met with me three or four nights a week at a local Irish pub to plan a spiritual renewal of our council.

During this time, he asked many questions that made me uncomfortable: Had I read the texts of the Second Vatican Council, or was I simply quoting what the SSPX says about them? How could I refuse to receive Holy Communion at the new Liturgy when it is the Liturgy Pope John Paul II celebrates? If I believed the Vatican II Liturgy to be valid, why not receive Christ daily? Was it not Satan who said *"non serviam"*[65] and Mary "Let it be done to me according to Thy word"?[66]

"What's the functional difference," he finally asked me one night, "between your private interpretation of Tradition and a Protestant's private interpretation of Holy Scripture? You both avoid the sacraments as a result."

I hated Eric's questions. They were a thorn in my conscience. They reminded me that the positions I had taken were ultimately untenable.

Saved from the remnant by obedience

Sure, the *Ecclesia Dei* movement had provided me with the Holy Eucharist through its reverent Tridentine Latin Liturgies, but I still couldn't bring myself to attend a Mass offered

[65] "I will not serve."
[66] Cf. Luke 1:38.

according to the post-Vatican II Liturgy of Pope Paul VI, let alone receive Communion there. In fact, if I found myself in a diocese where no Mass was offered according to the *Ecclesia Dei* indult, I'd simply stay home and not fulfill my Sunday obligation.

Deep within me spoke a quiet voice alerting me that something was amiss. In rejecting the SSPX schism, had I truly embraced the Church?

As part of a Catholic remnant, I continued in some matters to reject the Second Vatican Council, Pope Paul VI's liturgical reform, and the post-conciliar papacies. Like St. Paul, I believed I must resist St. Peter's to his face.[67] For a time, this eased my conscience, but then I was stuck asking myself why I had left both Protestantism and the SSPX. Would St. Faustina, in her message of Divine Mercy, resist St. Peter to his face? She was no St. Paul, and neither was I. Moreover, St. Paul never resisted St. Peter's *teachings;* he resisted St. Peter's actions when they were contrary to his own teachings as Pope. Reflecting on the example of St. Faustina, I realized that she, having placed her trust in Jesus Christ, would by extension trust in Christ's Vicar on earth. Were she living today, she would joyfully submit herself to Pope John Paul II, not resist him.

Yet I'd submit to no hierarchical superior whom I considered tainted by the liberalism of our day. I continued in this state until one day I happened across a passage written by the seventeenth-century French bishop Bossuet. Addressing the Jansenist[68] sisters of Port Royal during one of the Church's

---

[67] Cf. Gal. 2:11.

[68] Jansenism holds that man's free will is incapable of choosing what is morally good, and therefore any good that results from

battles with moral rigorism, he writes, "You are as pious as angels, but as proud as devils."

I saw in an instant that my rejection of the Second Vatican Council wasn't built upon the rock of Catholic Tradition, but upon the sands of pride. I had proudly placed my own doctrine above that taught by Christ's chosen Vicar.

With St. Faustina's message of Divine Mercy seeping into my soul, I saw clearly the difference between her merciful God reaching down from the Cross with pierced hands to embrace a fallen humanity, and the rigorist God of legalism, who grudgingly dispensed salvation to the handful of souls able to tread the exceedingly narrow path. I came to see the beauty of the Second Vatican Council's universal call to holiness, through which the Church calls every man and woman to sanctity.

I discovered that Catholic Tradition calls us, not to resist the Church, but to obey her and to pray for her.

Honoring Christ's presence
wherever it is found

Thus, my conversion back to Catholicism required that I place more trust in Christ's Mystical Body. Yet, what is conversion but a lifelong process through which we continuously come closer to Christ in His sacraments and in His Church? Fortunately, over the next five years, our Lord gave me the grace to work through various issues still impeding a full sense of trust in the Church.

Following my acceptance of the Second Vatican Council, I came to accept the validity and authenticity of Pope Paul VI's

his actions is predestined by God. Because Jansenists also tended toward an exaggerated strict moral discipline, in time Jansenism would come to denote moral rigorism.

liturgical reforms as mandated in *Sacrosanctum Concilium* — the Council's Constitution on the Sacred Liturgy. In paragraph 11 of that document, I read that the Liturgy, and in particular the Holy Eucharist, is the "source and the summit" of the spiritual life. Yet by avoiding the Liturgy of Paul VI when I wasn't able to attend a Latin Tridentine Mass, I had excluded myself from the "source and summit."

Ironically, my principal reason for avoiding the new Liturgy had been a statistic claiming that only thirty percent of Catholics believed in the Real Presence. Yet in refusing to honor our Lord's Real Presence in the revised Liturgy, was I not numbering myself among the seventy percent of nonbelievers? I knew I could no longer reject God's sanctifying grace just because it came through a Mass offered according to the revised Liturgy of Paul VI.

Jesus prayed for a man, not just an office

One last hurdle needed to be overcome: distrust of Pope John Paul II. I didn't doubt the legitimacy of John Paul II's pontificate, but I worried he might be too infected by modernism and liberalism to perceive a possible state of emergency within the Church. Despite the answers I had found in my canonical research, human doubt remained. My head knew the answer, but my heart was apprehensive.

However, I knew our Lord's divine mercy would eventually heal me of this wound. During my Christmas break in my last year of studies, a package arrived just as I finished praying the Divine Mercy chaplet. It was a Christmas present from the Benedictine priest who served as my new spiritual director. It was a few days early, but I cheated and tore off the wrapping paper. I saw before my eyes a copy of Hans Urs von Balthasar's masterful defense of the Roman Papacy, *The Office of Peter and the Structure of the Church*. Having just survived final exams on various sections of the Code, I was sick of Canon Law. I decided a little venture into ecclesiology — the theology of Church — would be a nice change of pace.

I picked up the book and began reading for a few hours, not really paying much attention. Suddenly, I came to a passage that stood out. In it, von Balthasar quotes Luke 22:31-32: "Simon, Simon, behold, Satan demanded to have you, that he might sift you like wheat, but I have prayed for you that your faith may not fail; and when you have turned again, strengthen your brethren."

What is interesting to note, but isn't distinguished in the English translation of this verse, is that this third *you,* as well as the *your* and *you* that follow, is singular. In other words, Satan had asked to sift *all* the Apostles like wheat; but Christ prayed specifically for *Simon Peter,* that *his* faith would not fail, so that he could strengthen the other apostles afterward.

I dropped the book as the distinction between Simon and Peter registered in my mind. God had preserved *Simon's* faith, that it might not fail. Our Lord guaranteed not only the faith of the Roman Pontiff, but of the man who held the office. Two thousand years later, was our Lord merely protecting the faith of Pope John Paul II, or was He also protecting the faith of Karol Wojtyla, who holds the office of Roman Pontiff? Stunned, I grabbed my chaplet and uttered, "Jesus, have mercy on me a poor sinner!"

At home on the foundation of Tradition

To this day, my former SSPX friends and acquaintances can't understand why I returned to Rome — believing themselves never to have left it. Of course, throughout the Church's history, countless saints and martyrs paid a much greater price than misunderstanding in order to safeguard their communion with the Church. Like these holy men and women, I trusted in our Lord to provide me sufficient spiritual strength to withstand such trials, and He was faithful. By His grace, I now embrace the whole of Catholic Tradition, including Christ's promise to St. Peter: "The gates of Hell will never prevail."[69]

As St. Faustina wrote in her diaries, "Jesus, I trust in You."

[69] Matt. 16:18.

A Baptist Lawyer Meets the Bride of Christ

Studying the Catholic Faith to get closer
to my Catholic girlfriend led me to a Bride
and to a union I never expected.

Br. Paul Campbell, LC

I had never considered Catholicism until I met Anne Marie. It started innocently enough: I was living in upstate New York in the fall of 1990 when a fellow attorney gave me her phone number. I called her. We took a walk through the neighborhood, and I discovered that she was beautiful, intelligent — and Catholic.

Although I was a faithful, active Baptist at the time — I had accepted Jesus as my personal Lord and Savior and taught Sunday school at my church — it didn't bother me too much that she was Catholic. I didn't think Catholics were totally lost, just wrong on some important points. In fact, I thought that no one church had the full truth. Particular churches, being filled with sinful human beings, were prone to error. Each denomination had elements of the truth and needed to teach and learn from one another. The truth about Christ, I thought, was like a mountain — too large to take in all at once. We had to gather the different churches and their unique perspectives to gain a better understanding of the whole mountain.

No, it didn't bother me that Anne Marie was Catholic. I was just happy to find an intelligent young lady who loved Christ and took her Faith seriously. But it bothered her that I was *not* Catholic. She was convinced that the Catholic Church had the fullness of truth, not just one of the portions that had been parceled out among the denominations.

Seeking unity in love and faith

Despite my initial thought that our religious differences didn't matter, over time I could see they did. Love seeks unity, but our disunity of faith divided us. As Anne Marie encouraged me to learn more about the Catholic Faith, I thought about this question of unity as it related to the many Christian denominations.

When I looked at Scripture, it seemed clear that God wanted Christians to be united. In the Gospel of John, Christ prayed for His disciples to be one.[70] Their oneness was to reflect the inner nature of God and to be a witness to the world of the truth of the Christian Faith. Paul was scandalized by the Corinthians who identified themselves with particular apostles, saying, "I belong to Paul," or "I belong to Apollos."[71] The Acts of the Apostles describes the original community of believers as being of one heart and mind.[72] If they were united in mind, their unity must have included shared doctrine.

In some Protestant circles, there was an effort to establish unity by "transcending" doctrinal arguments; they sought to be nondenominational, slimming down the Faith to what

[70] John 17:20-26.
[71] 1 Cor. 3:4.
[72] Acts 4:32.

everyone could agree on. Despite their good intentions, this doesn't work. Imagining away differences of belief can't build real unity among churches any more than it could build real unity in my relationship with Anne Marie.

I saw that division between Christians wasn't God's will, but what was I supposed to do? How was I to find my way, among the thousands of churches, to the one place where God wanted me? I had to find the answer to that question.

Corruption in the apostolic chain?

As a Protestant, I believed that at some point in history the early Church became corrupt, straying from the true Gospel message. I began to read some of the early Church Fathers to see whether they could show me when that happened.

I didn't find evidence of corruption in the Fathers. What I did find were distinctively Catholic ideas such as the Real Presence of Christ in the Eucharist, Apostolic succession, and the hierarchical structure of the Church. These doctrines are mentioned without dispute, as if they were simply part of the air Christians breathed. And these Catholic concepts were taught by men who had learned their Faith from the Apostles!

As a Protestant, I accepted Scripture as the Word of God. I didn't doubt that the Apostles faithfully transmitted what Christ had taught them. This was a necessary part of my Faith in the inspiration of Scripture: God inspired these men, and what they wrote was free from error. Thus, there was at least one necessary human link in the chain between Christ's message and its transmission in Scripture. If I were to accept Scripture as infallible, I also had to accept that God had given a kind of infallibility to the authors of Scripture — in the case of the New Testament, to the Apostles.

Still, it was difficult to accept that any man's teaching could be free from error. When Anne Marie spoke of papal infallibility, it struck me as arrogance. How could any mere man be infallible?

Yet, I began to see in the New Testament that within this gift of apostolic authority, priority had been given to Peter. Some of the evidence for it was subtle, such as his name invariably being mentioned first in lists of the Apostles.[73] Peter was part of an inner circle of three apostles chosen by Jesus to witness particular moments of His life, such as the Transfiguration and His agony in Gethsemane.[74] In the Acts of the Apostles, Peter appeared as the leader of the Twelve, announcing the need to find a successor to Judas.[75] He was the one who spoke on Pentecost.[76] He exercised a central role in the Council of Jerusalem.[77] He went to Samaria to verify the Samaritans' reception of the Gospel and to confirm them in the Holy Spirit.[78] Although Paul was the Apostle to the Gentiles, that there should be a ministry to the Gentiles was a specific revelation given to Peter.[79] To Peter alone were given the keys of the kingdom,[80] the task of strengthening his brothers in the Faith,[81] and the feeding of Christ's sheep.[82] What's more, the

[73] Matt. 10:2-4.
[74] Matt. 17:1; 26:37.
[75] Acts 1:15-26.
[76] Acts 2:14.
[77] Acts 15:6-11.
[78] Acts 8:14-17.
[79] Acts 10:1-47.
[80] Matt. 16:19.
[81] Luke 22:32.
[82] John 21:15-19.

first-century writings of St. Clement[83] — one of the earliest popes — were clearly authoritative in tone, demonstrating an acceptance of the authority of the Church and the papal office.

God mediates through created things

As a Baptist seeking to understand the Catholic Faith, I found the sacraments to be another problematic area for me. In my church, we didn't have them. Part of the reason is that Protestants seek to eliminate all intermediaries between God and the individual believer. We thought that God gave His grace directly to Christians through faith. There was no need for any mediation. I didn't need to go a priest to have my sins forgiven. I could pray directly to God, and He would forgive my sins. I didn't need water to be born again. All I needed was faith in Christ. When John recorded in his Gospel these words of Christ: "Whoever eats my Flesh and drinks my Blood," I understood them figuratively, without a second thought.

I've become convinced that Protestantism's anti-sacramental bent stems from a tendency toward a kind of Gnosticism. Gnosticism was one of the early heresies in the Church, one central idea of which was that matter is evil. Thus, a good God would neither create nor use material things. Now, most Protestants don't go so far as to believe that all matter is evil, but they can tend toward suspicion of matter and the body, of the interaction between the physical and the spiritual — hence, the Protestant aversion to candles, statues, incense, ornate churches and vestments, and the preference for radically simplified, spiritualized Christianity.

---

[83] St. Clement of Rome (d. c. 99), third successor to St. Peter and martyr.

However, this isn't biblical Christianity. God created the world and man essentially good.[84] Sin brought evil into the world, but it did not make the world evil. Moreover, from the book of Genesis through the book of Revelation, we see that God uses the mediation of human beings and material things to bring His saving grace into the world.

A perfect example is Moses. Moses was a mediator between God and Israel. God spoke to Moses, and then Moses spoke to the people in God's name.[85] God gave the Law through Moses. Even Moses, in turn, exercised his God-given authority through other men and material things. Aaron was appointed his spokesman.[86] Moses appointed seventy judges to govern Israel under him.[87] His staff turned into a snake to prove his authority.[88] He used his staff to divide the Red Sea and to strike a rock to bring forth water.[89] When he raised his staff in the air, his army was victorious.[90] When his people were dying in the desert, he made a serpent of bronze and raised it in the air so that they might be healed.[91]

We see the same thing in the New Testament. Jesus applied mud to a blind man's eyes and told him to wash in the Pool of Siloam.[92] A woman with the hemorrhage was healed when she

---

[84] Gen. 1:31.
[85] Deut. 5:22-28.
[86] Exod. 4:16.
[87] Exod. 18:24-27.
[88] Exod. 4:2-5.
[89] Exod. 14:16; 17:6-7.
[90] Exod. 17:8-13.
[91] Num. 21:9.
[92] John 9:6-7.

touched Jesus' cloak.[93] A paralytic was brought by his friends on a mat to see Jesus, but the house was full of people and they couldn't get inside. So they climbed onto the roof, made a hole in it, and lowered him down right in front of Jesus. Jesus saw their faith and said to the man, "Your sins are forgiven."[94]

That paralytic man wasn't healed by his faith alone. It required the faith and work of his friends, who believed in Jesus and took the initiative to bring him to Jesus. Matthew concludes his narration of the healing of another paralytic by noting that the crowd was struck with awe and "glorified God, who had given such authority to men."[95]

This is just a sampling of what I discovered in Scripture. The more I read, the more I saw there the principle of sacramental action, of God using human beings and material things to accomplish His plan of salvation. It is His habitual mode of action in salvation history.

Sacraments have power to effect what they signify

Not only could I see this sacramental principle in general, but I could also see its specific application to the seven sacraments.

Baptists don't believe that Baptism confers grace, but see it merely as a symbol or public profession of conversion. They believe that the faith of conversion is what justifies. As I continued to study, I began to see that this wasn't a necessary conclusion from Scripture.

---

[93] Mark 5:25-30.
[94] Mark 2:2-5.
[95] Matt. 9:8.

When Peter preached to the crowd on Pentecost, many believed. When they asked him what they needed to do to be saved, Peter responded in a distinctively non-Baptist way. A good Baptist would have pointed out that there was nothing they could do; they were saved by faith alone. They merely needed to accept the free gift of salvation by accepting Jesus Christ into their hearts as their personal Lord and Savior. But Peter didn't say this. He said, "Repent, and be baptized, every one of you, in the name of Jesus Christ for the forgiveness of your sins."[96]

Jesus told Nicodemus that no one could see the kingdom of God unless he was born again.[97] Nicodemus didn't understand what he meant, so Jesus solemnly declared, "Truly, truly, I say to you, unless one is born of water and the Spirit, he cannot enter the kingdom of God."[98] As a Baptist, I believed that I was born again when I accepted Jesus Christ as my personal Lord and Savior. Water wasn't part of the process. Yet Jesus spoke of water and Spirit.

Before ascending into Heaven, Jesus instructed the Apostles to make disciples of all nations, baptizing them in the name of the Father, the Son, and the Holy Spirit.[99] The ending in Mark provides this: "He who believes and is baptized will be saved."[100]

John the Baptist was in some ways a good Baptist. He preached. He called people to repent of their sins. He baptized

---

[96] Acts 2:38.
[97] John 3:3.
[98] John 3:5.
[99] Matt. 28:19.
[100] Mark 16:16.

adult believers by immersion in the Jordan River. However, he was a transition, not the point of arrival. As he baptized repentant sinners, he pointed toward another baptism, a different kind of baptism. He spoke of one who would baptize with fire and the Holy Spirit.[101] When I reflected on what I believed as a Baptist, I saw it as something more akin to the baptism of John and not to the baptism that John promised would come in Jesus Christ.[102]

"Scripture alone" leads to fragmentation

One of the battle cries of the Reformation was *sola Scriptura*: the principle that Scripture was the sole authority to arbitrate doctrinal disputes. It presupposed that the meaning of Scripture was plain and self-interpreting. However, my discovery in Scripture of a foundation for the sacraments was enough to show me that *sola Scriptura* doesn't work. Without a guiding authority, honest attempts to make Scripture the sole rule of faith always result in conflicting interpretations. As a *sola Scriptura*–observing Baptist, I had been trying to use Scripture for a purpose it was never intended to serve; I was trying to gather water with a net.

It's not enough to know Scripture. We must understand it. "How can I understand unless someone explains it to me?" cried the Ethiopian eunuch.[103] So God sent Philip to explain Isaiah to him. On the road to Emmaus, Jesus explained the meaning of the Messianic prophecies to two disciples.[104] Peter

---

[101] Matt. 3:11.
[102] Cf. Acts 19:1-5.
[103] Acts 8:31.
[104] Luke 24:27.

taught the first community of believers that Gentiles could become Christian without first becoming Jews.[105] Despite having received Christ's revelation directly, Paul went to Jerusalem to confer with Peter and to have his message confirmed.[106] Peter himself mentioned that some things in Paul's letters were hard to understand and that some individuals were misinterpreting them.[107]

Lacking a common authority to interpret Scripture, guided by fallible human preachers, theologians, councils, and traditions, Protestantism necessarily fragments, and fragmentation has continued to our own day. The historical result of the application of *sola Scriptura* is the existence of more than twenty-five thousand Protestant denominations, each claiming the right interpretation of a self-interpreting Scripture.

This is contrary to God's plan.

If we believe that it is God's will that Christians be of one heart and mind, we must also believe that God has provided a teaching authority. Only one common authority, preserved from error by God's grace, can keep Christians united in doctrinal matters, and the Catholic Church is the only church with a historical connection to the apostolic Faith that claims to possess such authority.

Old unions severed, new ones forged

At some point in my study and reflection, I began waving the white flag. My arguments were defeated, my misunderstandings clarified, and my questions answered. But intellectual

[105] Acts 11:1-18.
[106] Gal. 2:2.
[107] 2 Pet. 3:16.

conviction wasn't enough to bring me to the Church. The final barrier seemed to be emotional attachments — to my Baptist church and to my ministry with the youth there. I knew I had to leave the Baptist church, whether I joined the Catholic Church or not, and I didn't think it was right for me to teach Baptist youth in a Baptist church unless I believed in Baptist doctrine. So I resigned from my work in the church, and my emotional ties there began to weaken. Finally, after more than two years of search and study, I was ready to become Catholic — which, I thought, would surely please Anne Marie.

Then came the unexpected. Within a week of my firm decision to convert, Anne Marie called and broke up with me. She had met someone else and was ending our relationship.

I was devastated. I couldn't believe it. It was like being in a bad movie. She had been with me throughout my entire journey toward the Catholic faith, a little over two and a half years. She was the given, the constant. Suddenly, she was gone. I felt as if my life was unraveling, but I knew there was no going back. Once I had seen the truth, I couldn't close my eyes to it. I was going to become Catholic — not because I had a Catholic girlfriend, but because Catholicism was true.

Through the difficult days that followed, God held me together. God is good. He was pruning me. I knew it. I felt it, and I accepted it. I knew I had to become Catholic even though I didn't know what lay ahead of me. I certainly never could have foreseen my subsequent entry into religious life with the Legionaries of Christ. At the time, I felt like Abraham, when he was still Abram and God called him to go to a land He would show him.[108] He didn't know where it was. He didn't

---

[108] Gen. 12:1.

know what he would find when he got there. He just knew he was doing what God wanted.

From here things seemed to move very quickly. I began attending classes for those interested in joining the Church, taught by a spry, saintly parish priest approaching his eighties. I also remember a friend asking me whether I was going to become a priest. My reaction was "No way." I wanted a family. Although I had thought about being a Baptist minister since my teenage years, the priesthood was a different thing entirely. But the question continued to haunt me.

On the first Sunday of Advent in 1993, I became Catholic and learned that studying the Catholic Faith and being Catholic are two different things. Rather than reading about the grace of the sacraments, I was receiving that grace. It was like living in a different world.

From a career to a vocation

In January 1994, I began to pray about the priesthood. It was a simple prayer. "Lord, You know the desires of my heart. I offer them up to You to do with what You want." It wasn't an easy prayer to say. In offering God my plans and my desires, I was giving Him the freedom to do with them as He saw fit.

Over the course of many months, God turned my heart toward the priesthood. First I began to see the beauty of it. A priest is called to extend Christ's priesthood in time, to give His Body and Blood to the faithful, and to be an instrument for the forgiveness of sin. Then my own desire began to grow. I felt as if Jesus was drawing my heart toward Himself.

In November 1994, I was offered a partnership in the law firm where I worked, but I had to turn it down. I told them I thought God was calling me to be a priest and that I had to go and see. I didn't know what I would find, but I knew I had to go. So I wrapped up a career and started out on a vocation. I spent the following summer with the Legionaries of Christ, and I joined them in September 1995 as a novice.

As I ponder God's hand in my life, I'm amazed at His patience and goodness. Growing up, I could never have imagined myself as a priest. Now I can't imagine myself as anything else. The passage of time helps me to see God's Providence more clearly. He revealed His plan to me in bits and pieces, forcing me to walk very closely behind Him. I suppose if I could have seen too far into the distance, I'd have been tempted to stray off on my own. God's plan is always best.

Freed from Anti-Catholic Bonds

In ways large and small, God led me to the Catholic Faith
against the strong objections of my family — including my
brother, a prominent anti-Catholic writer and speaker.

Patty Bonds

I say unto you, unless you turn and become like children, you
will not enter the kingdom of Heaven."[109]

It was late September 2000. I sat at my computer under the
dim light of my desk lamp, typing an e-mail. My family was
asleep. I was alone with God and with the realization that I
was about to bring my life, as I had known it, to a sudden and
complete end. I had prayed for the right words with the right
spirit to explain briefly to a number of my friends what had
transpired over the last six months. The e-mail read:

Dear Friends,

Gen. 12:1 & 4a

"Now, the Lord said to Abram, 'Go forth from your
country, and from your relatives and from your father's
house, to the land which I will show you'; so Abram
went forth as the Lord had spoken to him."

---

[109] Matt. 18:3.

I understand in a new way how Abram must have felt when God came along and told him that life was about to change drastically. It is a very difficult thing to walk away from everything that has been familiar and comforting to you and to follow God into unknown territory, alone, with His words echoing in your ears and His guiding hand in yours. This is where I have been for several months now, and the time has come to make it known to all of you.

For the past six months, I have been studying the Catholic Faith.

I have found that "to be deep in history is to cease to be Protestant" (J. H. Newman). The discoveries I have made have been so amazing and such a surprise to me. It has been the most difficult, painful, confusing, enlightening, exciting, glorious six months of my life. If I had not had the previous five years of walking closely with God, learning to hear His voice and to respond in obedience even when it hurts, and learning that discipleship means death to self and to every form of strength and comfort outside of Him, I would never have been able to recognize His leading and to follow Him down this path (John 10:27).

I am thankful for all of you at Northwest Community Church and those friends from other churches who have been my friends and faith family. I love you all and hope that we can remain close. I will not be severing relationships. If this occurs, it will have to be the choice of others. I will not engage in arguments. I have watched too many of those and have come to the firm belief that such arguments and debates grieve the Lord.

I am attending church and classes at St. Helen's Parish. I have resigned from Northwest Community Church. My husband and family are supportive of this decision. They presently wish to remain at NCC, and I may be coming with them at times, but St. Helen's is my church home now.
God bless you all.

In Christ,
Patty Bonds

I read it over, prayed over it, and read it again. Now I sat silently with my heart beating rapidly and my hand trembling on the mouse. I asked God for His strength and comfort as I clicked "Send."

"There goes my life, Lord. There goes my family, my reputation, my ministry, my identity, and more than likely, my friends. For all I know, this may cost me my marriage. I need you, Lord. Hold me close."

"Saved" at six

I was raised in a Baptist family, the daughter of a Baptist pastor. My earliest memories were of sitting quietly in the front pew while my father led the singing and my mother played the organ. My mother and I sat together and absorbed my father's preaching. I knew the Bible stories from Sunday school by heart.

One Sunday in October 1962, not long after my sixth birthday, we had a guest speaker for a revival meeting at our church, a fire-and-brimstone preacher whose vivid description of Hell scared me. Suddenly I realized that when Jesus came to die for sinners, that included me! I was in need of a Savior.

At the conclusion of the sermon, my father closed the service with an invitation to anyone who had not come forward to stop at the door on their way out and tell him that they had decided that tonight was the night they wanted to give their lives to Christ and be "saved." I had been embarrassed to go forward at the altar call, but when the service was over, I made a beeline for my father, who was standing at the back door shaking hands with people. I walked up to him and said quietly, "Tonight is the night, Dad." He knew right away what I meant, so he abandoned the crowd and took my hand. We went to the front pew of the church and talked. He asked me a few questions to see whether I knew what I was doing, and then he gave me the words to pray a sinner's prayer. It went something like this: "Dear heavenly Father, thank You for sending Jesus to die for my sins. I know that I am a sinner and that I need a Savior. Please forgive my sins, come into my heart, and save me for Jesus' sake. Make me the kind of person You want me to be. Thank You for saving me. In Jesus' name. Amen."

I prayed along with my father, and then the hugging and tears began.

Two months after I prayed to receive Jesus, our family was blessed with an addition. I spent the evening with my schoolteacher while my mother and father went to the hospital for the delivery. That evening we got the call from my father, and he told me I had a little brother and that his name was James Robert.

The next summer, my father baptized me at a neighboring church. As I had been taught in the Baptist church we attended, I viewed my baptism purely as a gesture of obedience that had no effect on my salvation. Eternal life came instead from the act of placing my faith in God — after that moment, I believed, I could never lose my salvation, no matter what I did. I had received an "assurance of salvation," as it's often called by many Protestants. A person choosing to be baptized is thus already "saved" — a point many Baptist pastors like to emphasize.

Growing up anti-Catholic

I first heard of the Catholic Church when I was in grade school. I had a friend at school who came over to play at our house. She taught me to play "Go Fish" with cards that my parents didn't let me play with. We hid them in the shed. She taught me how to listen to modern music on the transistor radio. I'm not sure how my parents realized that my new friend was opening up a new world for me, but they put a sudden stop to our friendship. One of the reasons they gave was that she was Catholic.

I remember my mother explaining that Catholics believed they had to work their way into Heaven, that they prayed to statues, and that they said the same prayers over and over like pagans. She was particularly critical of the Pope and the idea that a man on earth would claim to be the head of the Church. She said that Catholics didn't think for themselves; they let the Pope think for them. They weren't even allowed to read the Bible for themselves. She told me that some children throw up when they take First Communion because it makes them sick to think about eating Jesus' Flesh. I could see the point. It was strange and sickening to think about eating someone's flesh.

What kind of people were these Catholics anyway? How could they believe such things?

At the time, my father was preaching a series of sermons on the book of Revelation. These sermons were captivating, and I looked forward to each Sunday evening's installment. I remember my father's saying that the "Whore of Babylon" referred to the Roman Catholic Church and that the Antichrist was the head of the Catholic Church, the Pope. I accepted that belief, and from that day on, I saw anything Catholic as evil.

As the daughter of a Baptist minister, I grew up in a home where theology, the Bible, and an intense emphasis on what it means to be "saved" (versus the state of being "lost" that Catholics and other "unsaved" people were in) was deeply woven into the fabric of our family's life. I entered adulthood firmly convinced that as a born-again, Bible-believing, Baptist Christian, I had the truth. Period.

Catholics, I had been taught and had come to believe, most definitely did not have the truth. And nothing could have convinced me otherwise.

Even in the midst of my devoutly Christian youth, I experienced some difficult challenges that would, in time, test my Faith in the Lord in ways I couldn't have foreseen. As many children do, sadly, I experienced some terrible things during my childhood that scarred me emotionally and spiritually. I was unable to trust God because I had developed a distorted image of Him. But God's grace never abandoned me and, although I didn't realize it yet, His healing was on the way.

Into Calvinism and counseling

I became Mrs. Richard Bonds in 1982. In 1985 Richard and I had our first child, Kimberly Anne. She was such a joy to us that we immediately wanted another. Sarah Nichole was born in 1986, followed by Esther Daniella in 1989.

In 1992 we left the Southern Baptist Church that my family had attended for many years. My brother James had left two years earlier for a Reformed church.[110] James shared with our family the virtues of Reformed theology, as he saw them, and Richard and I quickly grew more Calvinist in our views. We found ourselves arguing with other members of our Baptist church about issues such as predestination and free will. We came to have a very different perspective on life and evangelism. We also felt that we needed to be where we would be deeper in the Word of God than we were as Southern Baptists.

I asked James for his recommendation on which churches in our area we should attend. He suggested Northwest Community Church. Most of the elders and members there were of a Calvinist persuasion. We took his advice and switched to that church. We immediately felt more at home. Our senior pastor was more of a Bible teacher than a preacher. He taught the Bible using an overhead projector and outlines that he'd hand out to the congregation each Sunday. We spent months going verse by verse through different books of the Bible.

Yet even as Richard and I settled into our new church home, we began to suffer ever-increasing marital strife. The scars that I carried from traumas that I had experienced in my childhood were affecting our relationship. I reluctantly agreed to speak with a counselor recommended by our pastor. Along with her late husband, this woman had spent twenty years helping others. With their unique, biblical approach to

---

[110] "Reformed churches" are those Protestant churches, such as the Presbyterian church, that follow the theology of the Reformers Ulrich Zwingli (1484-1531) and, more particularly, John Calvin (1509-1564).

counseling — a "discipleship methodology" — they had successfully tackled just about every kind of problem.

In my bitterness, I was ready to quit before we even began, but I agreed to tell her about my marital woes. She listened for a while and then spoke to me about my own sinful responses to the suffering in my life. She told me that as Christians we are called to suffer; that our suffering brings about growth and increased Christlikeness. She told me that God can take the suffering of my life and make something beautiful of it, but only if I surrendered it to Christ and gave thanks in the midst of my pain.

That was a new perspective for me! Her words gave me hope that perhaps God had not failed me. I left with a clearer view of my own sinfulness and rebellion against God. I also left with the hope that God was not done with me. The following months brought me spiritual challenges I never thought I could face. They also brought deep healing, as God poured out His grace on my life and brought me peace. He gave Richard and me the tools we needed to begin the process of healing our marriage.

Shades of Catholicism in "discipling"

I learned things while studying this discipleship methodology that would later pave my way home to Rome. For example, we used confessors to assist in the process of healing. We were taught to make a thorough examination of conscience: not just what we did or didn't do, but what our motivations were, what our attitudes were, how we tried to control situations or people, how we responded to the sin of others in sinful ways, etc. We learned to delve into relationships and chronic sin situations and dig sin out by the roots. We made a detailed list of these sins and, in the presence of the counselor (or "discipler"), confessed them to God one by one. I found that this method for coming to terms with our personal sin and our attitudes toward others to be deeply biblical and Christ-centered. The disciplers were constantly amazed at the liberating effect of this method. It was apparent that confessing sin before a witness, someone older and more mature in the faith, was phenomenally effective in breaking patterns of sin and freeing people from guilt.

God in His infinite wisdom knew that, left to our own devices, we would deceive ourselves into believing that right was wrong and wrong was right unless we had accountability and authority involved in our examination of conscience and our confession of sin. I came to appreciate the power of confession of sin to a brother. I was yet to learn the grace of confession of sin to one who had been commissioned by Christ and His Church to forgive those sins in Jesus' name and to pronounce the beautiful words of absolution over me.

Another thing I was taught through this methodology was that true Christians lived lives of obedience and loving service. Belief alone was not evidence of salvation; obedience was the mark of a true Christian.[111] This was a new concept for me. It revolutionized my view of salvation. I no longer saw faith alone as the point of salvation. It was no longer a matter of mental assent, but of unconditional surrender to Christ, selfless love of others, rejection of sin, and following in Jesus' footsteps — in our relationships, in our conduct, and in our thought.

---

[111] Cf. Matt. 7:21-23, 18:21-35; Luke 6:46-49; 1 Cor. 13; James 2; 1 John 3:19-24.

My discipleship training taught me to live in the presence of God and to obey His prompting. I learned to trust God as I obeyed Him. I stepped out in faith and obeyed His commands even when it was extremely difficult. He showed Himself faithful. I grew to love my Abba more than my own life. The more I obeyed Him, the more I loved Him, and the more I grew to know Him.[112] He was as close as my own breath. I lived in a state of glorious fellowship with the Lord. Life was sweet. I was Abba's little girl.

My brother makes a name for himself

In the preceding years, my brother James had become deeply involved in studying theology and had for some time engaged in Protestant apologetics, focusing his conversion efforts on Mormons and Jehovah's Witnesses.

Then he turned his attention to the Catholic Church. Understandably, we were all proud of James as he sought to spread the message of Reformed Protestantism to Catholics and to show them that Roman Catholicism didn't represent the Gospel of Jesus Christ.

By 1998 he had earned a doctorate in Protestant apologetics and had written a number of books attacking Catholicism. He regularly engaged in debates with nationally known Catholics, including Tim Staples, Fr. Mitch Pacwa, Fr. Peter Stravinskas, Robert Sungenis, and even with the editor of this *Surprised by Truth* series, Patrick Madrid.

Even before he had grown prominent, I had listened attentively to the post-debate conversations James had with our parents at family dinners. I heard from him how this or

[112] John 14:21.

that Catholic had attempted to defend the Catholic Church's teachings from the Bible.

Theologically, I agreed with his arguments against the Catholic Church, but I didn't enjoy the intensity and rancor of those debates. I found them to be an occasion of sin for those on both sides. Tempers flared easily, and I just didn't see that arguing changed hearts. I preferred to spread my anti-Catholic beliefs by sharing my version of the Gospel with my children and my friends, and by living my life in love of God and in obedience to Him.

Those darn Catholic Irish

In the spring of 2000, my daughter Kimberly expressed an interest in learning more about our Scottish/Irish heritage, so we decided to go to the Scottish Highland Games in Mesa, Arizona. It was wonderful. The sound of bagpipes filled the air; Highland dancers defied gravity in competition and exhibition; genealogy experts helped us trace our family roots back to the old country. We learned about our clans and septs.

What a glorious day it was! It gave us both a strong sense of belonging. As we left the festivities that evening, we decided to investigate the Irish side of our heritage the following month at the St. Patrick's Day Parade in Phoenix.

As the parade began, a car carrying the Catholic bishop of Phoenix drove by; shortly after that, a retired priest who was obviously loved and honored by the Irish community. Then came the Knights of Columbus in full regalia. It was a "Who's Who" of Catholic life in Phoenix. I felt out of place. Why did these Irish have to be so, so *Catholic?*

At the end of the parade came the star of the show: St. Patrick himself, dressed as a Catholic bishop, complete with staff and what looked like a fish-shaped hat. I had been told somewhere in the past that the miters worn by bishops represented a pagan fish god. The sight of them always made my skin crawl.

I wondered how much truth there was in the legends about St. Patrick. When I got home that evening, I did some research on the Internet. I expected to find mythical tales about his sending all the snakes into exile in England; instead I found sites that treated him seriously, as though he were an actual historical figure.

One caught my eye: "The Confessions of St. Patrick." I thought it probably contained some juicy gossip about St. Patrick that the Irish might not want us to know.

But instead I discovered a Christian man of God who walked humbly with the Lord and who knew Him as well as I had come to know Him — or maybe even better! I discovered in St. Patrick a brother, a kindred spirit.

But how could a pagan Catholic bishop know the Lord Jesus Christ the way I did? How could there be this unity of spirit between St. Patrick, a Catholic, and me, a Bible-believing Protestant?

At that moment, the Holy Spirit awakened in me the need to know and understand the Catholic Faith.

Friends help break down my resistance

I was amazed and not a little concerned to notice that over the next few months, the Holy Spirit began a gradual process of warming me up to Catholicism. I had been raised so anti-Catholic that He had to break down formidable walls of prejudice before I could take a sincere, objective look at the Faith. God also started preparing my heart through music. My husband bought me a couple of CDs by an Irish Catholic singer whose songs reflected the rich Catholic heritage of Ireland. Usually I would have put such CDs in a cupboard or simply thrown them away. Because of what the Holy Spirit was doing in my heart, I cherished them.

I began asking questions of my two Catholic friends. Magdalen had a lively, active, and joyful faith. I had never heard a Catholic put such emphasis on faith in Christ. Brad had been my chiropractor for seven years. I knew he was Catholic, but I also knew he was a true believer in Christ. His life had been an example of charity and friendship. I knew he loved the Lord. This made him an oddity to me, and I simply refused to think about his religious affiliation because it did not fit into my theological stereotypes.

I asked Magdalen and Brad isolated questions to see what kind of answers I'd get. Then one day in Brad's office I began asking deeper questions. He said he was not much of an apologist, but he knew a book I should read. I bristled immediately and told him that I was a "*sola Scriptura* kind of person" and if the Catholic Faith was not scripturally sound, I wasn't going to consider it.

He smiled and assured me that it was indeed scripturally sound and that I just needed to read the book, called *Rome Sweet Home,* which he promised to get for me. I asked for a *Catechism* as well. I thought that if I was going to examine this Faith, I needed an authoritative resource, not merely a testimonial. He agreed.

At that point, with the exception of Magdalen and Brad, no one knew I was thinking about the Catholic Faith. And I certainly wouldn't have been caught dead buying a copy of the *Catechism of the Catholic Church.*

Drawn by the Eucharist

In late April 2000, still curious about how I could have so much in common with Magdalen, I was inspired. I thought if she came to *my* church, she would find she was even more at home there than she was in her church. At the same time, I was curious about what went on at a Catholic Mass. So I called Magdalen and suggested we visit each other's church. She agreed, and I made plans to attend my first Catholic Mass the next evening (which turned out to be Divine Mercy Sunday).

I was nervous as I approached the doors of the church, but once inside, I found that it seemed like a normal place. There were none of the medieval pictures or statues I expected. The walls were a familiar beige, and the decorating was of a South-western flavor. The baptistery was obviously for immersion, which made me feel more at home. I sat down and tried to be calm and relaxed.

As Mass began, I realized what a fish out of water I was. Everyone knew what to do — except me. There was so much bowing and gesturing! I tried to fight the tension building up in my neck and shoulders. After some pleasant singing, we sat down and a woman reverently stepped up to the podium and read a passage of Scripture. Hearing Scriptures made me feel more at ease. We sang a song I recognized as being derived from the book of Psalms. Just as I began to relax, the congregation stood and began singing. Then the deacon turned and bowed to the priest, who made the Sign of the Cross over him. He walked to the pulpit and read a passage from the Gospels.

So far, I was very impressed with how scriptural everything was. Even the sermon was quite good. I didn't understand the need for the formality and pageantry, but I could see why my friend's Faith seemed so biblical. She lived in a scriptural community of faith.

Then came the Eucharist.

I had no idea how my life was about to change. Without warning, the Presence of God fell on that place. I had never felt Him as powerfully as I did at that moment. I lost touch with most of what was happening around me. I barely kept up with the Liturgy. I stood there bathed in the light of God's breathtaking Presence. It went on and on as each of the parishioners filed forward to receive Communion.

As the Mass ended, I was speechless with joy at the Presence of God. I hugged my friend and said goodbye. I walked into the parking lot not able to feel my feet on the pavement.

I prayed frantically for answers. "What was that, Lord? I have to understand this. What do I do now? I know you want me to look into the Catholic Faith, but where do I begin? I'm not a theologian or a scholar. Where do I begin?"

His answer came immediately and unmistakably: "Start with what draws you; start with the Eucharist." I drove home knowing I would do just that, somehow, some way. I was excited . . . and afraid.

Catholic myths go up in smoke

While Brad was rounding up books for me, I tried to think of another way of getting information. I didn't know whom to trust. If I went to my extreme-Calvinist associate pastor, I knew what he'd say: "Run, repent, refuse to listen to those deceivers!" I knew where my brother stood, and I knew I wouldn't get unbiased information from him. So I prayed for wisdom.

Then I remembered a man I'd known years back, a man who'd become close to the Catholic Church, yet still held many of the same beliefs I did. Back then, I had been deeply moved by what he had to say, although I didn't understand why. I felt I could get some objective information from him, and since he lived so far away, I could avoid discovery by friends and family.

For the next month, this man sent me by e-mail Catholic doctrine on the Eucharist, justification, Purgatory, and many other topics. He gave me solid, objective information and endured my endless and often repeated questions — especially about the sacrificial aspect of the Eucharist. The documents he sent began to show me that the early Church saw the Eucharist, not just as a symbol or a memorial, but as the true Presence of Christ.

I was shocked by what I was discovering. Contrary to what I had been taught to believe by my Baptist friends and family, Catholics *weren't* cannibals; they didn't believe that Jesus was crucified over and over again on the altar; the Real Presence of Christ in the Eucharist was *not* a medieval innovation, but a thoroughly apostolic and biblical doctrine handed down from the earliest times.

The Catholic Faith was nothing like I had thought it was.

At that same time, Brad gave me the books he had offered me. I started reading *Rome Sweet Home* by Scott Hahn and his wife, Kimberly, both of whom were converts to Catholicism. I had never heard of a Protestant converting to the Catholic Church. I knew many who had left the Church to become Protestant, but I had never considered people of great faith, devotion to Christ, and academic excellence actually claiming to follow Christ *into* the Catholic Church. And Dr. Hahn had even been a respected, successful Protestant minister before his conversion!

I spent the weekend finishing *Rome Sweet Home*, and the theological foundations on which I had built my life cracked and could no longer support me. It was frightening and exhilarating at the same time: I was both thrilled by the possibility that Jesus was present in the Mass and terrified that I might have to leave the comfort of my doctrinal heritage and familial beliefs and venture into unknown territory, quite possibly alone.

I make a few friends in Heaven

On Monday morning, I woke up and realized that I had lost a small Celtic cross from my charm bracelet. I assumed I had lost it while walking my dogs the day before. When I walked them again later that day, I watched the sidewalk carefully. I loved that cross and wanted it back.

So I decided to test the Catholic waters a bit. I didn't know whether there was a patron saint of lost things or what his name might be, but I sheepishly prayed that if there were such a saint, he would pray for me and I would find that cross. But the cross didn't appear miraculously, and I soon lost hope of finding it.

I was tutoring that summer at a high school in an unfamiliar area. I didn't even know the name of the street it was on; I just watched for the parking lot and turned onto the street immediately after it. As I drove to work that Monday, I prayed out loud about the things God was doing in my life. I had just finished telling the Lord that if He was calling me to the Catholic Church, I would choose St. Patrick as my patron saint, because Patrick had led me there. Just as I uttered those words, I approached the school parking lot. The light turned red, and I had to stop. I looked forward as I waited for the green light. There before me was a street sign: Patrick Street!

Taking off my Protestant glasses

Summer school ended, and I had more time for reading. I decided that before I put my marriage, my family, and my whole life on the line, I would need to be sure of what I was doing. Even to have considered the Catholic Faith would be an embarrassment among my peers. It would have shown I had doubted our own rightness. I wasn't willing to damage my reputation.

I wanted to know that what I was studying was accurate. For example, in *Rome Sweet Home,* some of the quotations from the early Church were quite a revelation, and I wanted to know whether they were authentic. I had grown up mistrusting Catholics and anyone of a different belief system, including other Protestants. I needed to check the word of this Catholic convert to see whether he was quoting the early Christians honestly.

I looked up the writings of St. Ignatius of Antioch on the Internet. I will never forget reading his words concerning the Eucharist: "They abstain from the Eucharist and from prayer because they do not confess that the Eucharist is the flesh of our Savior Jesus Christ, flesh which suffered for our sins and which that Father, in His goodness, raised up again. They who deny the gift of God are perishing in their disputes." I gasped and pushed my chair back from my computer. "I've been robbed!"

After checking some of the other quotes I had read, I realized that my mistrust of Catholicism had been misplaced. I needed to question everything about Catholicism I had believed until then. It was time to take off the Protestant glasses.

I decided to test the direction in which I was heading by reading my brother's books against the Catholic Church. I knew of no other books with as strong an anti-Catholic message as his. I reasoned that if he could not refute what I had learned from the Bible and Christian history about the Catholic Church, it couldn't be refuted. I had recently finished reading his book challenging Catholic teachings on Mary. I took two of his other books off the shelf at home and began studying them, my Bible at my side.

I soon saw that James was fighting a caricature of the Catholic Church: his arguments attacked a misinterpretation of Catholic teaching. He did a great job destroying teachings he wrongly ascribed to the Catholic Church, but his anti-Catholic rhetoric left the real teachings of the Church unscathed. His characterization of the Eucharist as a repeated sacrifice of Christ demonstrated his ignorance of Catholic doctrine and an earthbound view of heavenly reality. You cannot repeat a sacrifice that exists perpetually in the eternal present of Heaven![113] He called the Sacrifice of the Mass a denigration of the finished work of Christ on the Cross, showing his failure to see that the Sacrifice of the Mass is Christ's finished work applied to our lives within the earthbound limits of time. Although examples of temporal punishment for sin fill Scripture, he denied the existence of Purgatory. His arguments against the Communion of Saints and devotion to Mary demonstrated a superficial understanding of the biblical evidence, as well as of the Catholic teaching that, in the Mystical Body of Christ, each of us is called to intercede on behalf of the others.

Rather than turn me away from Catholicism, my brother's books only confirmed and deepened my interest in it.

[113] Cf. Heb. 10:10.

Searching for peace at
the crossroads of a choice

Months earlier, I had attended a seminar on Catholicism presented by one of our associate pastors, who had been raised Catholic and later become a "born-again Christian." He had made up a chart to present what he believed the Catholic Church taught and the opposing Protestant position for each doctrinal point. I had kept the chart. Now I took it out to see whether it contained information that I was overlooking in my examination of Catholic teaching.

But rather than discovering fatal flaws in the Catholic position, I found that, even after just a few months of study, I could disprove each point this pastor attempted to make against the Catholic Church. I remembered how he and some in his audience had mocked the Catholic Church, and I shuddered at their ignorance and at their irreverence for truths I had begun to see so clearly.

After wading through more materials critical of the Roman Catholic Church, I became utterly convinced that the Catholic Church was right about these biblical and historical issues and that the Protestant arguments were wrong. I no longer had a choice. I had to embrace the Catholic Faith or run from the truth and go back to where I had been, and spare myself the struggle that lay ahead.

I was terrified and had trouble sleeping. I sought constantly to discern the truth. I prayed for God's guidance and protection from deception. I would wake up in the night debating with myself. I had troubling dreams about the opposition I would face if I embraced the Catholic Faith.

One of my prayers at that time was that God would give me peace and joy: peace of mind, so that I could think clearly without fear and confusion; joy, because the joy of the Lord had been my strength and I needed that strength now.

The Hahns lend a hand

While making dinner one night, burdened by discouragement, I prayed that God would send help. Then the phone rang. It was Magdalen. She asked whether I was all right. I smiled, knowing my prayer had been answered. I asked if I could call her back in a few minutes, made some excuse to my family as I set dinner on the table, and rushed to the bedroom to make the call. Magdalen was on the other line with her sister and asked if she could call me back later. I hung up. But the need to talk to someone was unbearable.

I took a long shot and called the Hahns.

The young lady who answered said Kimberly was busy with the baby and Scott was away. I left my name and number and lay face down on my bed, praying with all my heart that she'd call me back. Minutes later the phone rang. It was Kimberly.

I asked whether she had ever heard of James White. She had. Then I told her I was his sister. I could hear a soft gasp on the other end of the line.

Looking back, I can imagine her thinking that here she was, alone with the kids, late in the evening, probably tired, and she had James White's sister on the phone. I imagine she shot up a prayer for help.

I took in a big breath and, with the tears beginning to flow, I said, "I think God may be calling me to the Catholic Church!" Then I heard a louder gasp, followed by words of love and reassurance. For thirty minutes we talked about everything from sacraments to what Richard's reaction to my conversion might be.

At the end of our conversation, she asked whether she could pray with me. Although I was afraid of praying with a Catholic because I figured I wouldn't know how, I said I'd be happy to pray with her. She began, "In the name of the Father and of the Son and of the Holy Spirit," and my heart warmed at the sound of the invocation of the Holy Trinity. She prayed for me in love and concern that I would follow Jesus wherever He led me. She didn't pray that I would become a Catholic, but that God would give me peace and joy in my journey and make plain to me where He was leading.

Peace and joy.

I smiled through the tears. My constant prayer those past weeks was her prayer for me.

At the end of our conversation, I asked whether I could correspond with her and Scott to ask questions. She gave me the e-mail address of their secretary, Marie. She was a convert herself and a knowledgeable catechist. We began to correspond almost daily, and we still do. Marie not only answered all my questions, but she stood beside me through the tough times and prayed me through some of the hardest days of my life. She has proven to be a treasure as a friend.

Marie endured my endless and often redundant questions. At one particularly frustrating moment, she said, "Patty, you can enjoy the ballet, or you can study muscles!" She explained to me that the Faith is more than just isolated doctrines; it has an organic unity that makes it one perfect whole. I wasn't able to see that yet and still needed to scrutinize every teaching.

I break the news to Richard

The time had come to tell my husband what was going on in my heart. Our marriage had been a challenge; now I was going to make it more challenging. He had married a Baptist girl and intended to raise our girls as Baptists; now I was thinking of becoming a Catholic. Earlier in our marriage, we had both seen Catholicism as a false religion and would have been terribly disturbed if any of our girls had even *dated* a Catholic. Now I was standing on the banks of the Tiber, wondering whether I was going to have to cross alone — completely alone.

One afternoon I asked Richard to come into our room for a talk. I was terrified that the next few moments would see the end of our family.

I forced out the words to explain that I had been studying the Catholic Faith for several months and that I was discovering it was nothing I was raised to believe it was. I had discovered that the Catholic Church is far more like the early Church than ours was. I had read most of my brother's arguments against the Church and had not found them persuasive. I wanted to take classes at a local parish and learn more. What did he think?

I sat and trembled and waited for an explosion. I barely breathed as he stood and walked toward the door. Then he calmly said, "Do what you feel you need to do."

I could hardly believe my ears.

I pressed on.

"What if the things I learn make it necessary for me to convert to the Catholic Faith?"

He said again that I should do what I felt I had to do.

Like Abraham fearing that he might aggravate God by pushing for an even better answer, I tried one more question: "What if the elders of our church came after you to try to make you stop me?"

Richard turned and looked at me. "I'd tell them to mind their own business."

With that he left the room. I could barely believe it! The explosion had not come. I was free to search for truth and follow Christ wherever He led me.

In August we went on a family vacation. In the van, I had a lot of time to read and listen to tapes. I had taken along Scott Hahn's three-tape series on the Eucharist. I could hardly contain myself as I listened. I wanted so much to share what I was learning with my family!

I had also been reading Hahn's *A Father Who Keeps His Promises*. I spent a glorious afternoon finishing the book and seeing how, from Adam and Eve to the present day, God had reached out to humanity through His covenants. Salvation history stretched out before me like a huge schematic of God's love for mankind. I closed the book, walked out onto the balcony of our hotel room, looked up and, before the Lord and all the hosts of Heaven, declared, "I'm Catholic. I'm coming home!"

All the way home, I was both happy and afraid. The more I contemplated the ramifications of my decision, the more fearful I grew.

Could I bear to lose my friends? What if I lost Richard? Would he take our children? The joy of discovering Christ's Church was tempered by my realization of the suffering this discovery might be leading me toward.

God gives me signs of His preparation

Part of that joy also included an awareness of how God had been preparing me in advance to embrace Catholic teaching. As He had helped me see past *sola fide* — that we are justified by faith alone — God had led me to understand Purgatory for the most part before I ever recognized God's call to the Catholic Faith.

One evening, about two years before that fateful St. Patrick's Day, I was deep in prayer, meditating on Heaven. Heaven was my favorite subject, and I longed to be home with my heavenly Father. I was asking the Lord what it would be like to come home to Him — what it would be like to pass from this earthly life to life in Heaven. As I prayed, I saw God as the consuming fire, as Scripture describes Him. I imagined the light of His presence and the power of His Holiness. I saw myself, an imperfect human, leaving this world and moving Heavenward. As Heaven approached, the radiance of God's presence had the same effect that a fire has on an object that gets close to it. Eventually everything flammable ignited and burned away. All that was left was imperishable and pure. I could see myself passing from my imperfect state in this life to the brilliance of His presence with the smoke of all my imperfection trailing behind me as I flew to the arms of my heavenly Father.

I had seen the fires of Purgatory, and they held no fear for me. Whatever had to happen so that I could look Him in the eyes and be His forever was worth the pain. *Refiner's fire, come and consume this living sacrifice!*

When I read Scott Hahn's description of Purgatory in *Rome Sweet Home*, I recognized the vision I had years before. God had been calling all along. He had been making the way straight so that when He knew He could trust me with His call, I'd be able to look back and recognize His working in my heart over time.

For a long time, I had been looking for that Celtic cross on the sidewalks of my neighborhood. I grew weary of looking and decided to "compromise" with God. As I walked my dogs one night, I told the Lord that someone must have found my cross and picked it up or it must have been pressed into the hot asphalt long ago. Since the little cross had cost me only four dollars and I knew I could get another one, I asked the Lord to have someone give me four dollars so I could replace it. I'd pay the 28 cents tax, but I needed the four dollars from Him.

That evening I visited my mother and father. Just before I left, my mother walked up to me with four one-dollar bills and said they were "to help with gas or whatnot." I sat there unable to speak. She had fanned out the bills so that I could see that there were four of them. It was as though the Lord wanted to be very clear that someone was giving me four dollars just as I had asked. That night I went to bed smiling about God's answer to my prayer.

The next day, I turned my wallet upside down and poured my change out. There was exactly 28 cents. I thanked whoever it was in Heaven who had prayed for me, and I prayed that at the craft store there would be another cross like the one I had lost. There was. I bought it and took it home, figuring it was as close to a direct answer from the patron saint of lost things as I would get.

That night, as we were going to bed, my husband paused by the linen closet and asked, "Whose Irish cross is this on the shelf?" There it was — the original cross I thought I had dropped in the street!

My heart stopped, and I looked at my youngest daughter, who knew the whole story about my missing cross and the patron saint of lost things who had replaced my cross earlier that day. She asked me whether I had learned any lessons from this. I told her she had no idea what I had learned.

I clutched the cross to my heart and gave in to knowing I wasn't alone: I had friends in high places who prayed, and prayed well.

Thank you, St. Anthony[114] *(whom I now know to be patron of lost items). It's beautiful. They both are!*

With RCIA classes starting, I decided to attend the parish of my friend Brad. The first Sunday night I attended Mass there, I knew I had found my home. I had an unmistakable sense of being right where God wanted me.

My daughter Kimberly began classes with me, but eventually quit because of school conflicts and because she had trouble with the Church's teaching on the Communion of Saints: she just could not accept praying to "dead" people. She argued with her teacher in the high school RCIA class. In her frustration, she even wrote a letter to Scott Hahn asking questions about Liturgy and saints. (Her letter would become a blessing to me later.) I kept my promise not to make her become Catholic.

I let her walk away and committed her to Jesus and His pursuing love. He had found me and brought me home. He could deal with her.

On the trail of apostolic tradition

Even as I continued to embrace Church teachings, through my readings I also grew more comfortable with the Church's conception of her own authority.

Over the years, I had heard all sorts of mind-twisting excuses to explain away the authority of the visible, historical

---

[114] St. Anthony of Padua (1195-1231), Franciscan friar and Doctor of the Church.

Church. I had heard that there had been a secret congregation of Baptists hiding in the caves and surviving without a trace over hundreds of years until they could come out in the open after the Reformation. I had heard that the Catholic Church started out all right, but suffered corruption when Constantine became emperor and made Christianity legal. I had bought into the absurd theory that the pagan priests were without jobs, so they signed on as Catholic priests and introduced pagan idolatry into the Christian Faith. Now all these excuses seemed unthinkable in the light of the obvious Catholicity of the earliest writings of the Fathers.

One quick tour though Eusebius's *History of the Church* makes it clear that the Church has believed in the Real Presence of Christ in the Eucharist, in baptismal regeneration, in Purgatory, in Mary's role as the perpetually Virgin Mother of God and the New Eve, and all other Catholic teachings since before Constantine was born — in fact, since the Apostles walked the earth.

I tracked down every Catholic teaching that scandalized my Protestant mind, and over and over again I found them clearly present in the pre-Constantine Church writings. The *Catechism* that Brad had bought me and that had offended me when I started reading it, now read for me like a modern-language version of early Church writings.

I had once attended an organizational meeting that my brother held when he was assembling his work on the "King James Only" controversy. I remember his emphasizing how carefully the Scriptures had been preserved. What he overlooked was that those who had been so meticulous in preserving the Scriptures — the Catholics — had been equally meticulous in preserving oral traditions. They were one and the same truth. To read about Polycarp's[115] repeating from memory the things Christ had done and the teachings of the Apostles was a perfect example of how meticulously the early Christians guarded Sacred Tradition. Eusebius quotes St. Irenaeus of Lyons discussing his memories of learning at the feet of St. Polycarp: "To these things I listened eagerly at the time by the mercy of God shown to me, not committing them to writing, but learning them by heart. By God's grace, I constantly and conscientiously ruminate on them."[116] From dwelling in their writings, I was beginning to understand the mindset of the early Christians. It was becoming obvious to me that the Lord had left us a living and authoritative Tradition that eventually found expression in written form, but that it was the Tradition, written or oral, that was the Christian Faith. There was no real expectation in the early Church that we would ever govern our lives and worship strictly by the writings of the Apostles and their contemporaries. The early Christians had received the Faith in total as the apostolic tradition and were guarding it for all time. St. Irenaeus had no compulsion to write down what he had heard from St. Polycarp; he hid the word of God in his heart.[117]

At this point, I finally developed complete confidence in the teaching authority of the Church. I trusted those precious saints of God down through the ages who had guarded the truth and plumbed its depths to explain the mysteries of God

[115] St. Polycarp (d. c. 156), disciple of St. John the Evangelist; Bishop of Smyrna and martyr.
[116] Eusebius, *History of the Church*, Bk. 5, ch. 20; St. Irenaeus of Lyons (c. 125-c. 203), missionary, bishop, and Church Father.
[117] Cf. Ps. 119:11.

for future generations. O glorious reality, that there is in this world an ultimate authority to which Jesus delivered the truth and which has guarded that truth according to His promise!

Esther opens up

In late September 2000, I reached the point at which I couldn't hide any longer. There was no turning back. I sat in the dim light of my desk lamp late one night to compose an e-mail to my friends at Northwest Community Church that changed my life forever. Since all my family members attended other churches, I still had some time before my family discovered my plans, but it was only a matter of time before word would reach them. I wanted to tell them before they found out from someone else. Richard was on my side, and the home front was stable, so I felt it was time to speak.

On October 10, my daughter Esther and I went to get ice cream and have some girl talk. As we sat on the bench outside the ice-cream store, I asked her what she wanted to talk about. Expecting we would be chatting about her friends and school, I was surprised to hear her say, "I want to talk about the Mass." Only a month before, she had come to me crying, saying that she was trying to learn to be a Christian and now I wanted her to learn to be a Catholic. She was angry and confused at that time, and my heart broke; now she was sitting with me, eating her ice cream and calmly asking about the Mass.

I walked through the Mass for her and in terms that a twelve-year-old with a Baptist background would understand and explained what Catholics believe about the Eucharist. Her eyes lit up, and she took in everything I said. When I had finished, she told me she wanted to go with me next time I went to Mass.

I die to my mother

Later that day, we went to my parents' house with a gift for my mother's birthday. I wore a crucifix around my neck, and as we drove there, I hid it under my shirt. I had been doing this for some time, and so far it had kept my secret secure. I promised the Lord that this was the last time I would hide Him. I would write that letter to James and to my parents this week, and I would never again deny my Faith before them. It was a terrifying thought, but I couldn't live like this any longer.

We visited with my mother and father and an ex-Catholic friend of theirs. My mother had received a necklace for her birthday and was showing it to me. The subject of necklaces made her notice the chain around my neck and under my shirt. Before I knew what was happening, her hand was on my chain; she asked what I was wearing and pulled my crucifix from its hiding place. I knew that if she uncovered a crucifix (a good Protestant would never wear one) in front of her ex-Catholic, Baptist friend, it would be humiliating for her, so I placed my hand over my necklace and asked if we could step outside to talk. Esther shot out of her chair and headed for the door. Dread of the coming emotional explosion gripped us both.

When we were outside, my mother took hold of the crucifix and the St. Barbara medal that hung behind it. With a gasp, she cried, "Catholic? Why Catholic?" She dropped my necklace and grabbed her hair as though she would pull it out. I attempted to assure her of my love for her and for the Lord, but she wouldn't hear me. She wailed like a mourner at the bedside of a dead relative. She put her hands over her face and ran into the house.

Esther and I looked at each other, took each other's hand, and headed for the car. On the way home, Esther told me that now she knew I was right about the Catholic Faith, because she had seen me stand up for what I believed. My little one was coming home.

My parents informed James of my decision to convert to the Catholic Church. About a week later, I received from him the first in a string of scathing letters containing theological rebuttals and even some personal attacks.

Since my conversion, I've done my best to respond to some of his accusations and arguments, but their sheer numbers and his antagonistic tone have wearied me to the point that I now simply ignore them. I'm convinced that only God's saving grace and merciful love can quench the anger that fuels some Protestants' hatred of the Church.

As I wait for that blessed day, I'm content in the knowledge that in becoming Catholic, I chose the truth over error. When I abandoned the heresies of the Reformation, I embraced Christian orthodoxy. I did the right thing. It may be God's will that I suffer for a time for the sake of the Truth, but if that is His will, I accept it. I will continue prayerfully to offer up my suffering for the sake of my brother's conversion to the truth.

Confirmation from my old pastor!

Reactions to my letter began to come in. For the most part, people just faded out of my life. Two ex-Catholic friends had some cold words (one of them was good enough to apologize months later).

Then the associate pastor of my former church called and asked to meet with me. We made an appointment. I was nervous because, although I had answered my own questions about the Catholic Faith, I was very new at defending what I had come to believe.

In his office, I tried to explain what had happened to me over the past several months. He made two comments that encouraged me. I'm sure he didn't mean for them to encourage me, but they were some of the strongest reasons to become and stay Catholic that I have ever heard. At one moment of frustration with me, he said, "Patty, you can read Scripture from the vantage point of the Reformation, or you can read Scripture from the vantage point of Tradition."

I just smiled. He was right. I could interpret Scripture through one of the thirty-two thousand perspectives the Reformation had created, or I could interpret Scripture in the one light of the Church's Tradition.

Later he mentioned that he had received an e-mail that contained proof that the Catholic Church hadn't changed her position on soteriology — the theology of salvation — in two thousand years. This time, my grin was obvious. What a glorious thought! I was embracing truth that had never changed from the beginning! My smile must have let him know he wasn't affecting me in the least, so he brought our meeting to an end, and I left, rejoicing.

Nothing warm and fuzzy about it

I've received many reactions from Protestants to my conversion. One that makes me chuckle is the claim that I am simply a victim of emotionalism: that I became Catholic because it made me feel warm and fuzzy or some silly notion like that. Had I intellectually *understood* the biblical issues, the claim goes, I never would have been so foolish as to embrace the unbiblical "Gospel of Rome."

The misguided people who have told me this have no idea how I agonized over my decision to become Catholic. Fear and loneliness were the predominant emotions that characterized my months of biblical study, scrutiny of Church history, and prayerful discernment. These are hardly emotions that would *entice* someone to choose the Catholic Church. In fact, I struggled *against* my emotions — which were telling me to not become Catholic because of the upheaval and pain it would cause in my life — so that I could objectively weigh the evidence for Catholicism.

Beholding my Mother

One day my mother called my husband to beg him not to let our children enter the Church. He told me about it that evening, and I remember feeling betrayed in my heart. I remember standing in the kitchen that evening doing my chores and crying out to God in the silence of my soul: "Why can't she understand? Why can't she trust me to follow You? I dread her wrath, Lord. I need a mother."

His answer to my prayer interrupted my thoughts: "You have one."

I knew He was referring to the Blessed Virgin Mary, whose role in the Faith I was just beginning to consider. I knew that it was time to come to terms with my Mother Mary.

In November my husband surprised me with the dream of my life — a trip to Ireland. I had longed to go to Ireland since I was young. I could hardly believe we were actually going to set foot in the places where my older brother Patrick had proclaimed the gospel and faced off with the druids 1600 years ago.

I asked Marie for information on Mary to fill the time on the plane and to help bring me peace about this subject. My brother's book on Mary made it sound as if the Catholic

Church made Mary the fourth member of the Godhead. He insisted, as many Protestants do, that Mary's mediation usurped the one mediation of Christ. I had developed confidence in the teaching authority of the Church, but I still was uncomfortable with the concept of Mary as a mediator. I had been raised in a "Jesus and me" environment. Any involvement in my relationship with God by anyone other than Jesus seemed like an encroachment on His unique place. Yet I never hesitated to ask others to help me interpret Scripture, to intercede for me in prayer, or to help me bear my burdens. I had relied heavily on my brother and my pastor for interpretation of Scripture. I had trusted only those sources they endorsed. I read the Bible translation they suggested. Yet the concept of Jesus' Mother praying for me or carrying my prayers to the Lord was disconcerting.

I prayed the entire Rosary for the first time on the plane en route to Ireland. I felt awkward and wasn't certain that thirty thousand feet in the air was the best place to risk offending God by praying to His Mother. It probably wasn't the best time to scandalize Richard, either, so I hid my beads under a blanket while I prayed.

In early 2001, my friend Marie wrote in response to my new love for Mary:

> I was thinking of how the doctrine on Mary as Mediatrix is something that even faithful, thinking, practicing, cradle Catholics often have a hard time wrapping their understanding around. God just really seems to be going straight to the core and turning your whole life around from the inside out. It's just so much like God to go lovin' after a Calvinist Baptist with our

Blessed Mother. And I mean in a way that He reveals her in such an evident, obvious way. Sometimes our Lady's role is more like Saran Wrap — we see straight through her to see Jesus more clearly, so much so that we hardly notice she's there. But it is a different grace altogether when the Lord says, "Behold, your Mother." Whoa! That's heavy-duty incarnational reality. God has some restitution going on in your life. To the one from whom much was despoiled and plundered, the gaze of God goes most directly, and the holiest help He gives.

Warm welcomes and cold criticisms

January and February were filled with study and a deepening of my faith. My daughter Esther was also growing to love the Faith and was becoming devout. On days off, we would get up early in the morning to go to eucharistic adoration. Her awareness of Jesus' Presence in the Eucharist amazed me. Her spontaneous response to His nearness proved to me that she wasn't coming home just to be with her mom; she was coming home to be with her Lord.

Early in February, I joined the Internet discussion group of the Coming Home Network. As a new member, I was asked for my testimony. I had seen only about thirty people taking part in the discussion so far, so, figuring it wasn't a very public forum, I felt safe in divulging my story without word getting around. That wouldn't be the only time I underestimated the Internet grapevine. My story was cut and pasted and sent to several Catholic apologists. I began getting e-mail from people who had debated my brother in the past. I was amazed at their tender attitudes toward a man who had been such an ardent opponent. Many of them told me that they prayed for him regularly and had for years.

What a difference from the spirit of war waged in the name of Protestant theology! In fact, in my Protestant days, I never saw that kind of patience, respect, and unconditional love for those of another faith. We Baptists had always had a kind of patronizing pity for those of other faiths, but never such self-giving love.

Two letters that arrived the same day underscored this difference. My daughter Kimberly got a letter from Scott Hahn addressing her questions in a warm, loving manner and advising her to take her time and just follow Jesus with all her heart, wherever He led her. That same day, a letter came to me from my brother, harsh and critical of my conversion. He suggested that a person would have to be mentally unsound to become a Catholic. I kept the letter that was full of the grace and love of God. What a picture God had painted for me of the reality of 1 Corinthians 13. Without love, we are empty noise.

In March I began to sense a real struggle brewing in my husband. I think he had been sure that if I studied long enough, I would change my mind about this Catholic stuff and settle back into a Baptist point of view. Now it was obvious that that wasn't going to happen. I could see his agony. I feared he would forbid me to enter the Church or to bring Esther with me.

Not sure what to do, I made an appointment with Fr. Louis, my dear friend and spiritual counselor and the associate pastor of our local parish. I sat in his office and bore witness to what God had done in my life and in my daughter's life. He stopped me occasionally during my story to ask me whether I realized what an amazing gift of grace I had received. I assured him that

I did. Then I came to the big question: What should I do if my husband decides to forbid me to come into the Church? Fr. Louis didn't hesitate: he said that it was God who had revealed to me the truth of the Catholic Faith, and for me to live any other way would be, not only a lie, but a serious sin. He assured me that there might be a terrible price to pay for my decision to follow Christ, but that I would have to pay that price if need be.

I knew he was right. I prayed the day would come that my husband would see what I saw and come to love the Faith I loved, but I would come home with or without him.

About a month before the Easter Vigil, I received a package from two of my former best friends, containing a letter and a Bible study. The letter itemized the reasons they felt I was in sin and rebellion from God because I was becoming Catholic. They accused me of becoming Catholic to establish an ungodly identity separate from my identity in Christ.

I had indeed lost my identity: most of my relatives and friends saw me as a rebel and a fool. But what I was going to gain eventually was my true identity — that of a precious daughter of God. Conversion is a death-to-self experience. But no one has left home or family or friends for the cause of Christ who has not been repaid a hundredfold.[118]

So full of grace

My first confession was a wonderful experience. For years I had been confessing my sins before another person, so I was spared the usual terror many people have. I think the most profound moment for me was when I confessed my part in

[118] Cf. Matt. 19:29.

propagating the Protestant Reformation. At first, my priest didn't want to hear that as sin, but I made it clear that it meant a lot to me to confess it. I was so relieved to be able to receive absolution for my sins, including my rebellion against the Catholic Church.

On March 26, 2001, the Feast of the Annunciation, I knelt before our portrait of Our Lady of Guadalupe in our adoration chapel with my friends Mimi and John, who had come to witness my Marian consecration. I used the prayer of consecration suggested by St. Louis de Montfort. When I came to the line "This day, with the whole court of Heaven as witness, I choose you, Mary, as my Mother and Queen," I began to weep from the depths of my soul. I was coming home *with* my Mother. What joy!

The time came for Esther's first confession. She was nervous. We decided to spend time in adoration before going to Reconciliation. Her discernment of Jesus' Presence in the Blessed Sacrament had always amazed me, but this evening it was obvious in a new way. When we arrived at the chapel, her little heart was angry about having to suffer "humiliation" before a priest. She could not sit before the Blessed Sacrament in that angry state. She took her paper and pencil and stood around the corner, out of sight of the monstrance, until her list was finished and she had surrendered to going through with the sacrament. Only then was she able to sit with me and adore Him.

When she came out of the confessional, she flew into my arms with happy tears streaming down her face. She looked up at me and exclaimed, "I feel so graceful — I mean so full of grace!" She wanted to know when we could go to Confession again!

Agony of anticipation, sweetness of fulfillment

For 233 days, I had been counting down to the Easter Vigil. As the number shrank to two digits and then to just a handful of days, the agony of not being able to receive Communion was as intense as it had been months before — painful in an almost physical way.

Holy Thursday came, and Esther and I were awestruck at the solemnity of the Mass. At the end, our parish priest took the Eucharist in the ciborium in his arms, wrapped it carefully in his vestments, and carried it from the sanctuary. A sense of emptiness swept over me. My daughter looked up at me and whispered, "Mom, now it feels like a Protestant church in here." Indeed, it did feel like the churches I had been accustomed to attending before God called us home. I ached for the Presence of Christ to return to the tabernacle.

Good Friday finally came, and the crucifix was laid on the floor at the foot of the altar. We each took our turn venerating the crucifix, patiently waiting for each person in attendance to have a moment to thank Jesus. I knelt and kissed the feet of Jesus on the crucifix.

I wasn't adoring wood and paint. When my lips touched the surface of the crucifix, my heart and soul were adoring Jesus Christ, my Savior and Lord, crucified, risen, and interceding for me. I had learned the value of sacramentals and of images that help us visualize and sense the presence of those in Heaven. I had gone from being put off by people who touched statues while praying, or who kissed images, to one who could hardly pass a statue of our Blessed Mother without touching Mary's hand and closing my eyes in order to spend a moment expressing my love for her and asking her intercession for me and for my family.

At long last, Holy Saturday arrived. It was a beautiful, sunny day here in Phoenix, and I could barely contain the joy of knowing that there were only hours between us and home. With the exception of a minor wardrobe problem at the last minute, the hours passed by without a hitch. My family arrived and seated themselves in the church while Esther and I stood outside with the newly lit fire. The celebrant lit the candle, and we followed him into the darkened Church, bringing the light of Christ.

The vigil Mass was unbelievably beautiful. Esther and I both heard our saints invoked in the Litany of the Saints. I thanked St. Patrick for his intercession and his testimony that opened my eyes and eventually brought me home. After the catechumens were baptized, it was time for our profession of Faith. Esther and I and several others stood to declare to all those who were there that we believed that the Catholic Church was the true Church that Christ established to be the preserver of truth. Moments later, we each filed to the front to pronounce our patron saint's name and be confirmed in that name. What a joy it was to hear the priest confirm me as a Catholic in the name Patrick. I bear it proudly and with gratitude. We stood again and approached the altar. Finally, after months of intense hunger, Esther and I received the Lord Jesus Christ on our tongues and into our beings, the way He had meant for us to receive Him.

Oh, for a thousand tongues to sing my great Redeemer's praise!

God spills grace all over my house

During a conversation with Kimberly Hahn a couple of months earlier, she mentioned that when Esther and I began receiving the sacraments, the grace we would be receiving would spill out onto the other members of our family. She was right. It wasn't long before my daughter Kimberly overcame her anti-Catholic prejudice and began asking good questions and accepting the things she was learning. My husband started to ask an occasional question and eventually started studying for himself.

God had made it very clear from the beginning of my journey that I needed to stay quiet and let God handle my husband's conversion, if there was to be one. I knew I was not to preach or try to persuade him. I was to love him and live a Catholic life before him. Now it seemed possible that I might win him without a word.

By October 2001, my husband had begun to study in earnest. He sometimes spent entire days closed in the bedroom with a book. He began meeting one-on-one with my book buddy and RCIA teammate, Bob. Richard is a quiet man, and for many months, the only indication I had that anything positive was happening was that he continued to study and meet with Bob. He and our daughters began going to Mass with us. Richard wouldn't kneel or genuflect or cross himself; he sat in silence and observed. I was just thankful he and the girls were there. We were a family in the pew, and it meant the world to me.

After Richard had spent months in silent study, I found an opportunity to ask him what his reaction was to what he had read. He told me that he had come to the point of accepting the Church's teaching on the Real Presence of Christ in the Eucharist!

I was thrilled. I felt prompted to tell him that St. Augustine taught that not only was it not sin to worship the Host, but it was sin *not to*. I could see that made an impact on Richard.

The very next Sunday, as we filed into the pew, I glanced behind me just in time to see him genuflect and cross himself. I managed not to burst into tears, but I was the happiest woman in the world.

Before I knew it, I was at a Confirmation retreat watching my husband bear witness about how thankful he was that I had boldly lived the Faith in our home and introduced the Bonds family to the Roman Catholic Church.

The other night, Richard had to write about his journey as an assignment for RCIA class. After quite a while alone in the bedroom, he came out and asked whether I thought what he had written made sense. I cried like a baby when I read his words. He had been so quiet, rarely giving me a glimpse into his heart, but with these few words, the reality of his conversion became crystal clear to me.

He wrote:

Although I have spent over forty years in a Protestant Church and felt God's presence in my life, I always felt that something was lacking. I don't believe that these forty years were wasted in my growing relationship with God; on the contrary, they served as stepping stones to lead me closer to the Father Almighty and to His Son, Jesus.

My wife, Patty, having been obedient to God's leading, caused a light to go on in my head that created a desire to investigate the Catholic Church. Having read several books, listened to several tapes, conversed with my wife, and after attending several Masses, I could discern quickly that my journey was finally leading me to cross the Tiber River. I was coming home to Rome!

For a cradle Catholic, this probably seems uneventful. For me, however, it feels like scales have been lifted from my eyes, and now I can finally see the richness of the intimacy of Christ during the celebration of the Eucharist in the Mass.

I do not take this journey lightly, nor do I take it for granted. I would not have crossed the Tiber River if God had not given me the faith to reach out to Jesus so that He could gently lead me across!

My new journey is now just beginning. Already it is full of mystery, anticipation, and wonder. If I was able to be obedient to God's leading me to the Tiber, then with the grace of God, He will provide me with the faith necessary to continue my journey after having crossed the Tiber into Rome!

Thanks be to God!

On March 5, 2002, Richard and I stood and took wedding vows before the altar at our parish and brought our marriage home in preparation for Richard's confirmation. Our girls did the readings and carried the rings. Sarah was accepted as a catechumen a couple of weeks later. Richard and Kimberly entered the Church soon after, at a joy-filled Easter Vigil.

Having the Catholic Faith in common has brought Richard and me even closer. It has also given us a different approach to raising our children. We don't see our daughters' salvation as a one-time event; we see it as something we need to help them nourish every day with the goal of building a foundation that will enable them to endure to the end. Because our conversions came so late in their childhood, we share a sense of urgency in teaching the Faith before they are grown and gone.

May you have light to see and courage to act

As I look back on my life, I can see the hand of God leading and healing and bringing me ever closer to the fullness of His truth. I thank God for the rich heritage of Scripture and moral teaching that my parents gave me. I'm especially thankful for the lessons in discipleship I learned from those at my former church who not only helped me heal from my past, but also taught me how to follow Christ even when it meant going it alone.

The ultimate test of how well I learned the lessons they taught me came when I had to follow Christ as He led me in a direction they considered unthinkable. I don't blame my parents for the anti-Catholic things they taught me. They were taught the same things by their parents, who were taught the same things by their parents — all the way back to the Reformation. I believe we are judged on the basis of the light we have, and my parents have been given only limited light.

Even as I write these words, furious opposition from my brother continues. One of his main accusations has been that, before becoming Catholic, I didn't listen to tapes of his debates; therefore, I wasn't really informed about the problems with Catholicism. My response is that I was well aware of his positions and arguments against Rome, partly because I had studied his written material, but mainly because I grew up in that same milieu. I was raised to believe in the same doctrines and have the same attitudes toward Rome that he did.

Nonetheless, I decided that I should take up his challenge of listening to his debates against Catholics. I have to admit now that I regret that I didn't listen to them sooner. Had I heard these debates, there's no doubt that I would have converted to the Catholic Church years earlier.

I challenge you who are outside the Catholic Church to take off your Protestant glasses and read the writings of the early Church Fathers and the Scriptures in the light of the time and the culture in which they were written. Lay aside your prejudices and fears. Be open to the glorious possibility that God did indeed establish a visible Church and entrust to her the truth of the Faith. Be open to the fact that two thousand years later, He continues to keep his promise to lead the Church into all truth.

It was frightening for me to take off those glasses, to consider that perhaps what I had believed all my life had been based on errors passed down for generations. Conversion is death to self. I was keenly aware that I was ending the life I had known to follow Christ.

But how could I walk away from the truth about Catholicism that had been revealed to me? How could I walk away from the Jesus I loved? How could I not run to receive Him now that I knew he was truly present in the Eucharist?

I could not be like those in John 6 who walk away from the One who has the words of eternal life.[119] I had come to the point where nothing else in life mattered as much as being nestled in the bosom of the Church that Christ established, nourished by His precious Body and Blood.

O taste and see that the Lord is good. Happy is the man who takes refuge in Him.[120]

---

[119] Cf. John 6:66-68.
[120] Ps. 34:8.

Why Are So Many
Non-Catholics Surprised by Truth?

Patrick Madrid

Over the years that I've worked as an apologist, I've had the privilege of getting to know hundreds of converts to the Catholic Church. I've long had a deep interest in the details of their journeys, a hunger to discover the mysteries of how grace worked in their lives and how God in His Providence arranged people, places, and things to draw them homeward.

What is it about Catholic truth that "surprises" non-Catholics enough to usher them into the Church? There are, of course, countless means at God's disposal to open the locked door of the human heart, but I want to mention a few that stand out in my mind as favorites of His.

Authority

In every conversion, there is that shining moment when the convert perceives the truth about authority. As converts have told me, in an instant what had been shrouded in darkness and obscurity becomes clear and certain.

Let's say you were raised an Evangelical Protestant whose whole life has been ordered around the principle that the Bible is the sole, sufficient, infallible rule of faith. No pope, no council, and definitely no "tradition" can vie with Scripture as an equal authority. Your entire theological outlook is predicated on the Reformation principle of *sola Scriptura* — by Scripture alone. Everything you believe is contained explicitly in the pages of Scripture, and anything that isn't contained therein must be rejected as a "tradition of men."[121]

But at some point, the lightning flashes and you see things not just in a different light, but as they really are. You see what's *really* there, as opposed to what you had always thought was there. You discover that Tradition — authentic Tradition[122] that comes from divine revelation, not mere human opinion — is indeed an integral part of the Christian Faith. The flash of illuminating grace might strike while you're reading a book of conversion testimonies or while attending a parish apologetics seminar and hearing the biblical case for the Catholic Church for the first time. It might come while you're driving to work listening to a Catholic apologetics tape or in a conversation with a Catholic friend that shows you from the facts of Christian history — *and from the Bible itself* — that Scripture was never intended by Christ to be the sole, sufficient rule of faith for Christians.

"And immediately something like scales fell from his eyes, and he regained his sight. Then he rose and was baptized, and took food and was strengthened."[123]

When a non-Catholic, especially a Protestant, becomes aware that the Bible isn't (and doesn't claim to be)[124] the sole rule of faith for Christians; that Sacred Tradition is not just a

---

[121] Cf. Matt. 15:6-9; Mark 7:6-8.
[122] 1 Cor. 11:2; 2 Thess. 2:15.
[123] Acts 9:18-19.
[124] Cf. 2 Pet. 1:20, 3:16.

corrupt Catholic version of the child's game "Telephone," but rather the Church's lived understanding of the original deposit of Faith; that Christ established His Church, not as a Bible-only fellowship, but as a teaching Church[125] endowed with His own authority,[126] the solution to his most urgent problems has been found. The authentic role of Scripture in the life of the Church is finally understood; Scripture is understood in the light of Sacred Tradition and connected to the teaching office of the Church's Magisterium; years of prejudice, misunderstandings, and suspicion toward the Catholic Church fall away.

No wonder men and women are still willing to enter the Church, even when it involves the loss of things they hold dear: friends, a job, influence in their community, perhaps even family members!

"The kingdom of Heaven is like a merchant in search of fine pearls, who, on finding one pearl of great value, went and sold all that he had and bought it."[127]

History

In the 1960s TV series *Dragnet*, Detective Joe Friday's classic line was "Just the facts, ma'am." Many converts to the Catholic Church take the same approach in their investigation of the claims of Catholicism. They don't want anti-Catholic hype, or legends and surmises, but just the facts. Happily, the historical evidence that verifies the authenticity of the Catholic Church as the one true Church established by

[125] Cf. Matt. 28:20.
[126] Cf. Matt. 16:18, 18:18; Luke 10:16.
[127] Matt. 13:45-46.

Jesus Christ is wide and deep. The facts of Christian history demonstrate overwhelmingly that the ancient Church was the Catholic Church.

Once a non-Catholic recognizes the continuity of doctrine and practice between the Church of the early centuries and the Catholic Church today, it becomes impossible to cling to the view that the Catholic Church is a "medieval invention" and that his form of Protestantism is closer to the Christian Church found in the pages of the book of Acts.

People reach that discovery by asking the same simple, honest questions: What doctrines and practices did the Christians of the first five centuries believe and teach and defend? How did *they* understand Scripture? How do the beliefs of the Catholic Church of the twenty-first century compare with those of the second century?

When they find the objective answers to these questions, the claims of Protestantism evaporate like the morning mist. To use the words of the great John Henry Newman (a brilliant English Protestant scholar and clergyman who converted to the Catholic Church in 1845), "To become deep in history is to cease to be Protestant."

The opposite of Newman's maxim is equally true: "*Not* to be deep in history is to *cease* to be Catholic." And we can help win back to Christ many fallen-away Catholics, especially those who have gone over to Protestantism, by showing them the evidence that the original Christian Church was the Catholic Church.

In no way do I mean to suggest here a sort of *sola historica* model for conversion, as if merely acquainting oneself with the historical evidence would be itself enough motivation to join the Catholic Church. Prayer and reflection, studying

Scripture, and a sincere openness to God's will are all required ingredients. But when those elements are present, especially openness to the truth and a willingness to be led even "where you do not want to go,"[128] the power of the historical evidence is felt most fully.

Beauty

I've met men and women who were not initially persuaded by biblical and historical evidence for the Church. They found themselves unmoved intellectually, but stirred inside when they encountered Catholic art or architecture. A simple crucifix, the calming resonance of Gregorian Chant, the soaring arches of a medieval cathedral — these and countless other expressions of spiritual beauty have been enough to melt hardened hearts when theological argument has failed to.

The Holy Spirit has many instruments of grace at His disposal and, as many converts will tell you, He often uses the power of beauty to open the locked door of the heart, revealing Himself through created things.

"Your eyes will see the king in his beauty; they will behold a land that stretches afar."[129]

I've heard some non-Catholics scoff at converts to Catholicism who admit that they were attracted, at least in part, by the beauty of Catholic Liturgy, art, or architecture. They scoff because, in their estimation, it's stupid to convert to Catholicism just because you like the "smells and bells" of Catholic worship. And in a sense they're right. But I've never met a convert, nor do I think one exists, who converted simply because

---

[128] Cf. John 21:18-19.
[129] Isa. 33:17.

of a fondness for the external beauty of Catholicism. I *have* met many converts who say that what really drew them was Truth, expressed through beauty. God's grace works through things that are aesthetically beautiful in the Catholic Church as a means of leading us to the real reason for conversion: the One who is Himself the way, the Truth, and the Life is found in fullness only within the Catholic Church.

Beauty has a unique power to unlock hearts and melt opposition to the truth. One morning, while on a recent speaking tour of universities and parishes in Germany, I was traveling by car through the city of Cologne, accompanied by a young American priest. His father, he explained, had been stationed in Europe during World War II as a bombardier on a B-17 Flying Fortress. As we drove toward the center of the old city, the priest pointed to the majestic spires of the cathedral off in the distance.

"My dad was flying a bombing mission over Cologne," he explained. "His plane had been ordered to strike military targets in the vicinity of that cathedral. The Allied bombing campaigns had reduced most of the city to rubble, but the spires of that cathedral still stood amid the devastation of the bombs."

I could picture in my mind's eye a young airman crouched in the forward compartment of the big bomber, squinting into the bombsite as he prepared to release another wave of fire and steel on the city below. The priest told me that his dad was a devout Southern Baptist, a Protestant who never had a very high opinion of the Catholic Church.

"Just as the plane came within range of the target, my father suddenly saw the spires of the cathedral standing in the center of what looked like a city-size pile of rubble. In that moment, somehow, a special grace of God flooded his soul. As he gazed down on the beautiful and ancient Catholic cathedral, he felt a luminous sense that there, in that church, in spite of the devastation that surrounded it, dwelt the presence of God. He was struck by a profound longing, a desire to know more about the Catholic Church."

Soon afterward, the airman converted to the Catholic Faith, and now, years after that remarkable incident, he has a son who is serving the Church as a Catholic priest. God can use such encounters with beauty, however fleeting they might be, to pour out His grace into a receptive soul.

After all, God is unsurpassed beauty itself, and He lavishes beauty on His friends and on all their works that glorify Him. The beauty of created things radiates the beauty of the Lord Himself, the way the moon reflects the light of the sun.

The Eucharist

Patty Bonds, whose conversion testimony is in this book, described to me not long after her conversion her first encounter with Christ in the Eucharist. It was the first Mass she had ever attended, and although she found the Mass to be beautiful and moving as it led up to the Eucharistic Liturgy, she wasn't expecting, nor was she prepared for, what happened at the Consecration.

She told me how "the presence of God fell upon that place," in a way that was so powerful and so moving that she was transfixed in a daze of love and gratitude to Christ. That phrase "the presence of God fell upon that place" struck me forcefully and has been an excellent reminder to me of the power of the Eucharist to draw souls to Christ and the Catholic Church. The fact that so many cradle Catholics — including me at times, I must confess — are often unfazed by the awesome power of Christ's Presence in the Eucharist, Body, Blood, soul, and divinity, is something that should sadden us, but we should be grateful to God for converts, for they remind us that Christ is truly present in the Most Holy Sacrament of the altar.

In his own excellent memoir of conversion, *Evangelical Is Not Enough,* my friend Thomas Howard recalls those times when, as a child, he would wander into an empty Catholic church during the day. He described how, even then, he could feel the presence of God in that place. It was the Eucharist he felt. Later, as an adult, he began to ponder the question: What is it that Christ wants most for us? Is it just fellowship? Just preaching? Just the Bible? What does Christ want to *give* us?

Tom discovered the answer to that question through the Eucharist. He discovered that what Christ wants most to give us is Himself. "I came that you may have life, and have it abundantly."[130] He who is Life itself, gives us life through the Eucharist. Thomas Howard discovered that fact in the dim quietness of an empty Catholic Church; but that church wasn't empty, for Christ was there, waiting for Tom, just as He waits there for each one of us. When converts discover the Real Presence of Christ in the Eucharist, they are drawn to it inexorably.

" 'The bread of God is that which comes down from Heaven, and gives life to the world.' " They said to Him, 'Lord, give us this bread always.' Jesus said to them, 'I am the bread of life; he who comes to me shall not hunger, and he who believes in me shall never thirst. . . . Truly, truly, I say to you, unless you eat

[130] John 10:10.

the Flesh of the Son of Man and drink His Blood, you have no life in you; he who eats my Flesh and drinks my Blood has eternal life, and I will raise him up at the last day. For my Flesh is food indeed, and my Blood is drink indeed.' "[130]

Personal example

Another friend of mine, Jesse Romero, is a former Los Angeles police detective who is now a well-known Catholic apologist and speaker. Recently he told me about an experience he had with a former Protestant police colleague who was very anti-Catholic. For years Jesse and this man would debate the question of the Catholic Church. It seemed to Jesse that the more they argued, the further this fellow moved away from the Church. He was frustrated because he felt as if he just couldn't get through to his Protestant coworker. Eventually, their running argument ended when Jesse retired from the department.

Years passed. Jesse then got a phone call from a mutual friend who told him that this same Protestant police officer was going through a bitter divorce and that his wife had kicked him out of the house. With nowhere to go, he was reduced to sleeping in the police-station locker room. Jesse hung up the phone and immediately drove to the station to meet his old friend.

"You can come and stay at my house, man," Jesse told him. "There's no way I can let a friend and fellow officer live like this. Come on."

His friend at first resisted Jesse's invitation, worried that it would be an imposition on his family, but in the end he relented and brought his stuff over to Jesse's house. The man

[130] John 6:34-35, 53-55.

lived with them for the next six weeks, eating with the family and enjoying a happy, stable home life. At no point in those six weeks did Jesse attempt to discuss religion with him. It was difficult to avoid it, Jess told me, but he bit his tongue and tried his best to be a good friend and to expect nothing in return.

Each evening before eating dinner, the Romero family prayed grace. Before the kids went to bed, they prayed their evening family prayers. Each morning, Jesse and his wife would bundle the kids into the family van and head to daily Mass. His friend watched but said nothing. He didn't go with them to Mass, and they didn't push him to.

Six weeks later, he took Jesse aside and with tears in his eyes, he said, "You've been so good to me, letting me stay here. And I really appreciate that. But you also haven't gotten in my face about your Catholic beliefs. You've left me alone on that and didn't push it. I appreciate that space, man. Over the last several weeks, I've watched how you live. I can see that you and your wife are raising your kids with Jesus Christ as the foundation for your family. You're happy and fulfilled, and you clearly love the Lord."

Jesse was humbled and grateful when his friend said that none of his other friends had opened their homes to him. Only a *Catholic* had — someone he had assumed for so long was "unsaved" and on his way to Hell. Jesse was overjoyed to hear his friend's next words.

"I want what you have," he said. "I know I've been really antagonistic in the past toward the Catholic Church, but based on what I've seen in you and your family, I feel a deep call from God that the answer is in the Catholic Church. Will you show me what to do to start learning?"

Why Are So Many Non-Catholics Surprised by Truth?

As Jesse told me this story, I could see a smile of gratitude and wonder at God's grace at work in that man's soul. "I didn't have to say anything to him!" Jesse exclaimed. "I just tried my best to live my life as a witness to Christ. And that's what God used to bring this man home."

Not long after his conversation with Jesse, the man entered the Church and is now a devout, Bible-believing, on-fire Catholic who reaches out to other Protestants with the message of Christ in His Church. One remark he made that still sticks in Jesse's mind is "I never realized that you Catholics really do love Jesus, until you showed me that love through your generosity and friendship when I was going through a rough time."

St. Francis of Assisi[132] once exhorted, "Evangelize always. When necessary, use words." Jesse Romero did exactly that, and God worked powerfully through him. The Lord wants to do the same through you. Ponder the words of Christ, and let them enkindle in your heart a renewed desire to reach out to non-Catholics and former Catholics with the burning charity that comes from knowing Jesus in prayer and the sacraments.

"You are the light of the world. A city set on a hill cannot be hid. Nor do men light a lamp and put it under a bushel, but on a stand, and it gives light to all in the house. Let your light so shine before men, that they may see your good works and give glory to your Father who is in Heaven."[133]

I ask you to consider prayerfully and often the power of the things that God uses to draw people to Himself. Look for

[132] St. Francis of Assisi (1182-1226), founder of the Franciscan Order.
[133] Matt. 5:14-16.

239

opportunities to help others encounter them in their journey toward Christ and the Catholic Church:

◆ The Truth about authority, the Bible, and the authority of the Church Christ established;

◆ The power of beauty and the way in which Catholic art and architecture reflect the beauty of God in profound ways that penetrate the mind and soul, speaking the language of love through symbols and signs that stir our very souls to approach God;

◆ The undeniable, objective facts of history: the early Christians weren't proto-Protestants, but Catholic in belief, worship, and practice;

◆ The reality of Christ's Presence in the Eucharist: there can be no middle ground on this point. Either Christ is not present in the Eucharist, in which case the Catholic Church can't be the true Church because she claims that He is; or Christ really is present in the Eucharist, in which case all men and women should become Catholic, for it is there that they will truly encounter the Lord most fully and have the deepest, most powerful "personal relationship with Jesus Christ" imaginable;

◆ And reflect often on the immense power of living an authentic personal life of virtue and Christian charity. This is something you can begin doing right now in your effort to love your neighbor as yourself. Pray for him. Edify him with your good example. Don't be showy or ostentatious in your Catholicism. Be humble and genuine. Show him that you really do love Jesus, and prove it by how you reach out in Christian love to him.

Feeding the hungry, giving drink to the thirsty, and clothing the naked are all things we are commanded by Christ to do, and for which we will each be examined and judged on the Last Day.[134]

We can understand that command in three ways. First, we are called literally to feed, clothe, and attend to the needs of our brothers and sisters.[135] Second, we are called to clothe the ignorant and uninstructed with the garments of truth; to give drink to the spiritually thirsty by leading them to the One who alone can slake their thirst for the truth.[136] Lastly, we are to feed them with the Bread of Life and Truth.

When we do these things, physically and spiritually, we help our non-Catholic friends to see the truth, to embrace the truth: to be joyously *surprised* by the truth.

---

[134] Cf. Matt. 25:31-46.

[135] "Bear one another's burdens, and so fulfill the law of Christ" (Gal. 6:2).

[136] Cf. John 4:5-15.

Recommended Reading

M any Catholics and others inquiring into Catholicism have found these books helpful. Those that are still in print are available from your local bookseller or can be purchased from Sophia Institute Press® (1-800-888-9344).

APOLOGETICS

All Generations Shall Call Me Blessed, by Francisco Manelli. Scriptural foundations of Catholic teaching on Mary.

Any Friend of God's Is a Friend of Mine, by Patrick Madrid. An introduction to the saints: Why do Catholics pray to dead people (saints)? Why don't they just go directly to God? Isn't praying to saints clearly a violation of the scriptural tenet that Jesus is the only Mediator between God and man? This book is a treasury of definitive biblical answers to these and many related questions about the Communion of Saints.

Catholic for a Reason: Scripture and the Mystery of the Family of God; Catholic for a Reason: Scripture and the Mystery of the Mother of God, edited by Leon J. Suprenant, Jr. These two volumes comprise an excellent introduction to Catholic teaching, especially for those who want solid, meaty explanations. Key Catholic doctrines — such as those on the

Mass, the sacraments, Purgatory, and Mary's role in the Church — are explained clearly and convincingly, showing the biblical reasons for being (or becoming) Catholic.

Catholicism and Fundamentalism, by Karl Keating. This is an essential guide to the Fundamentalists who have made it their mission to attack the Church and to draw the faithful to their sects. It shows how they misunderstand and misrepresent Catholic teaching and gives carefully reasoned answers to their charges and claims.

The Hidden Manna, by Fr. James T. O'Connor. Fr. O'Connor shows that the Church believed in the Real Presence from the beginning and that the Protestant idea that the Eucharist is symbolic is a late innovation.

Mary and the Fathers of the Church, by Fr. Luigi Gambero. This survey of the patristic period shows that Catholic teachings about Mary are nothing new, but are part of the very foundations of the Church and her message for the world.

Not by Scripture Alone, by Robert Sungenis, Patrick Madrid, et al. This book shows the errors in the core Protestant idea that Scripture alone is the rule of faith for Christians. It aims directly at Protestantism's Achilles' heel — and scores a direct hit.

On the Development of Christian Doctrine, by John Henry Newman. This monumental work by the famous convert from Anglicanism shows how doctrines develop and how to distinguish a true development from a doctrinal corruption. Newman demonstrates that the Catholic Church in its modern form is the only Church that has developed, organically and consistently, the principles of the apostolic Church.

Pope Fiction, by Patrick Madrid. Madrid provides clear answers to the objections non-Catholics raise to the papacy and its God-given authority in Christ's Church. Everyone who has been confronted by non-Catholics and ex-Catholics who claim that the papacy is a human invention, not a divine institution, will find this to be a comprehensive, informative handbook.

Search and Rescue, by Patrick Madrid. Madrid shares proven methods for reaching out to family and friends who have strayed from the Faith. Rooted in prayer, charity, and common sense, the advice in this book will help you pave the way for God's grace to work in the hearts of your loved ones.

The Scriptural Roots of Catholic Teaching, by Chantal Epie. You don't have to remain silent anymore when Protestants and other non-Catholics tell you (or your kids) that Catholic teachings go against the Bible! When your Evangelical Protestant brother-in-law Larry visits or Scripture-quoting Fundamentalists knock on your door, reach for this comprehensive, user-friendly guide that shows you where to find all the Church's major teachings in Scripture — especially the ones that non-Catholics most often contradict. Epie reveals the scriptural foundations of all the most important and most often controverted teachings of the Church: the source of divine revelation, the founding of the Church by Christ Himself, His establishment of the sacraments as means of grace, and the importance of devotion to Mary and to the saints.

Surprised by Truth 3

Surprised by Truth, edited by Patrick Madrid. A few of the converts whose stories are told here dabbled in the occult. Several were Protestant ministers. Some tried drugs. Some looked into Eastern religions. But eventually, by the grace of God, they were all confronted with the only thing that can satisfy the human heart: they all came to see the truth and saving power of the Catholic Faith. Their stories are encouraging, inspiring, and helpful in winning new converts.

Surprised by Truth 2, edited by Patrick Madrid. This second volume of the best-selling series of conversion stories gives you an insider's view of the belief systems that beckon to unwary Catholics: Fundamentalism, New Age paganism, Mormonism, and others. These stories will bolster your own faith when anti-Catholic arguments make you start to doubt, and help you convince your family and friends to become — and stay — Catholic.

Where Is That in the Bible? by Patrick Madrid. This book delivers fifteen years of apologetics experience in a condensed "treasury of Bible verses." Madrid surveys more than forty doctrinal issues — including the Eucharist, Purgatory, the papacy, and Mary's role in the Church — that are commonly misunderstood or even denied by non-Catholics. He provides lucid commentary and scriptural evidence for each section, showing how to explain and defend the Faith.

Why Is That in Tradition? by Patrick Madrid. This handy sequel to the best-selling *Where Is That in the Bible?* delivers the historical evidence for the teachings of the Catholic Church on some fifty apologetics topics, from the Eucharist to salvation, from the papacy to Mary and the saints. It includes a detailed explanation of exactly what sacred Tradition is (and what it's not) and shows how Catholics can share the truth of Tradition more effectively with Evangelical and Fundamentalist Protestants, Mormons, Jehovah's Witnesses, and others.

Winning Souls for Christ, by Fr. Raoul Plus. This book shows how to make yourself and the gospel message attractive to unbelievers, how to prepare spiritually to spread the gospel, how to handle rejection and discouragement, and how to win souls the way Jesus did.

BIOGRAPHY

Heroes of God, by Henri Daniel-Rops. This book introduces you to some of history's most courageous saints: men and women who suffered hardship and trial to spread the Faith and serve the poor. You'll come to know these saints as models for holy living and as powerful friends and intercessors in Heaven.

THE CHURCH

A History of the Church (three volumes), by Philip Hughes. This lucid, highly readable work invests Church history with high drama as it demonstrates how God has guided and protected His people and His message throughout the centuries.

DOCTRINE

The Aquinas Catechism, by St. Thomas Aquinas. St. Thomas had a remarkable ability to communicate the Faith — its most complex as well as its simplest elements — in plain language. Here you'll find his deeply insightful, straightforward, clear explanations of the Apostles' Creed, the Commandments, the Sacraments, the Lord's Prayer, and the Hail Mary. In other words, this book will give you a basic course in the Catholic Faith, taught by the Church's greatest theologian.

The Catechism of the Catholic Church. Pope John Paul II calls the *Catechism* "a sure norm for the teaching of the Faith." It is the authoritative source for what the Catholic Church teaches.

Fundamentals of Catholic Dogma, by Ludwig Ott. Ott presents Church teaching in outline form, with the connections between doctrines clearly delineated and the relative importance of each teaching noted. This is an essential reference for every Catholic.

The Spirit of Catholicism, by Karl Adam. Adam shows how the Catholic Church is not just a human society, but the continuation of Christ's work on earth. You'll come to understand how seemingly disconnected doctrines — such as the primacy of Peter, the Communion of Saints, and the sacraments — all flow from the central truth that the Church is the Body of Christ. This beautiful book has won scores of converts, including Scott Hahn, Dorothy Day, and Thomas Howard.

THE MASS

Preparing Yourself for Mass, by Romano Guardini. This book helps converts (and cradle Catholics) deal with right and wrong expectations of the Mass, overcome obstacles to

prayer at Mass, and learn the right — and wrong — ways
to receive Communion, to make the sign of the Cross, and
to perform other gestures that are part of the Mass.

PRAYER

The Art of Praying, by Romano Guardini. This remarkable
book offers practical ways to improve your prayers today.
In it, Msgr. Romano Guardini discusses particularly important issues for converts, including the right way to vener-
ate the saints, the importance of the Rosary, and much
more.

The Rosary of Our Lady, by Romano Guardini. In these illuminating pages, Guardini explains clearly and simply why devotion to Mary is appropriate for all Christians and shows
how repetition of the prayers in the Rosary — when done
properly — is the ideal form of Marian devotion. He explains each of the mysteries of the Rosary and suggests
themes for deeper meditation.

THE SPIRITUAL LIFE

The Secret Diary of Elisabeth Leseur, by Elisabeth Leseur. This
diary kept by Elisabeth Leseur for years is a helpful book for
converts who find themselves — as she did — feeling isolated among their non-Catholic family and friends. Leseur's
atheistic husband ridiculed and denigrated her Catholic
Faith. When he discovered her diary after her death, he
was so moved that he became a Catholic — and eventually a priest. *The Secret Diary of Elisabeth Leseur* is an essential guide for all those who must bear with attacks on their
Faith.

PERIODICALS

Envoy magazine. Here is a helpful resource for cradle Catholics as well as for those new to the Church. This award-winning bimonthly journal of Catholic apologetics and evangelization, edited by Patrick Madrid, presents the Faith in ways that will help you explain and defend it effectively, especially to those new to the Church or to persons inquiring into the Faith. (*Envoy*, P.O. Box 585, Granville OH 43023; 1-800-55-ENVOY; www.envoymagazine.com).

Biographical Note
Patrick Madrid

Patrick Madrid has been active in the full-time apostolate of apologetics since the late 1980s. His articles and essays in defense of Catholic truth have appeared in many national Catholic publications. To give faithful Catholics a resource they could turn to again and again for answers to challenges to the Faith, he founded the award-winning *Envoy* magazine, which has become one of the foremost Catholic journals of apologetics and evangelization.

He has also written and edited a number of books that explain and defend various aspects of the Faith; these include *Surprised by Truth, Surprised by Truth 2, Any Friend of God's Is a Friend of Mine, Pope Fiction, Not by Scripture Alone* (which he co-authored with Robert Sungenis), *Search and Rescue*, and *Where Is That in the Bible?*

In addition to writing on apologetics, Madrid has conducted hundreds of apologetics conferences in English and in Spanish across the United States, as well as in Europe, Asia, Latin America, and the Middle East. He's a veteran of numerous public debates on religious issues with Protestant ministers, Mormon leaders, and other non-Catholic spokesmen.

Patrick, his wife, Nancy, and their eleven children live in the countryside of central Ohio.

How to Contact the Contributors

Greg and Julie Alexander
The Alexander House of Austin
3610 Shell Road
Georgetown, TX 78628
beige@earthlink.net

Patty Bonds
P.O. Box 39074
Phoenix, AZ 85069
crossedthetiber@hotmail.com
www.soverygrateful.com

Br. Paul Campbell, LC
pcampbell@legionaries.org

Pam Forrester
1536 Green Canyon Lane
Fallbrook, CA 92028
pforrester1@aol.com

Paul Fox, M.D.
1006 Hamilton Avenue
Latrobe, PA 15650
pdfox@earthlink.net

Dwight Longenecker
29A Lowden
Chippenham SN15 2BP
ENGLAND
Dwight@longenecker.fsnet.co.ok

David Mills   ·
Trinity Episcopal Schl. for Ministry
311 Eleventh Street
Ambridge, PA 15003
davidmills@tesm.edu

Carl Olson
969 Nadine Drive
Heath, OH 43056
carl@envoymagazine.com

Monsignor Stuart Swetland
604 E. Armory Avenue
Champaign, IL 61820
msgrswetland@
newmanfoundation.org

Pete Vere, JCL
Peter_vere@yahoo.com

Tell Us Your Own Story

Did you recently join — or return to — the Church? Consider sharing with others your journey of faith!

We invite you to submit your conversion story for possible inclusion in future *Surprised by Truth* volumes. Your account should be true and should — persuasively, yet charitably — give the reasons that led you to become Catholic.

Please send manuscripts to:

Surprised by Truth Conversion Story Acquisitions
Sophia Institute Press
P.O. Box 5284
Manchester, NH 03108

Sophia Institute Press®

Sophia Institute® is a nonprofit institution that seeks to restore man's knowledge of eternal truth, including man's knowledge of his own nature, his relation to other persons, and his relation to God. Sophia Institute Press® serves this end in numerous ways: it publishes translations of foreign works to make them accessible to English-speaking readers; it brings out-of-print books back into print; and it publishes important new books that fulfill the ideals of Sophia Institute®. These books afford readers a rich source of the enduring wisdom of mankind. Sophia Institute Press® makes these high-quality books available to the general public by using advanced technology and by soliciting donations to subsidize its general publishing costs. Your generosity can help Sophia Institute Press® to provide the public with editions of works containing the enduring wisdom of the ages. Please send your tax-deductible contribution to the address below. We also welcome your questions, comments, and suggestions.

For your free catalog, call:
Toll-free: 1-800-888-9344

Sophia Institute Press® ◆ Box 5284 ◆ Manchester, NH 03108
www.sophiainstitute.com

Sophia Institute® is a tax-exempt institution as defined by the
Internal Revenue Code, Section 501(c)(3). Tax I.D. 22-2548708.